D0064725

The Ambivalent American Jew

The Ambivalent American Jew

POLITICS, RELIGION, AND FAMILY IN AMERICAN JEWISH LIFE

Charles S. Liebman

The Jewish Publication Society of America
Philadelphia
5736 / 1976

Small portions of this book have previously appeared in print. The author is grateful to the editors of the publications listed below for permission to reprint revised sections of the following articles:

"A Sociological Analysis of Contemporary Orthodoxy," *Judaism* 13 (Summer 1964): 285–304.

"Orthodoxy in American Jewish Life" and "The Training of American Rabbis," *American Jewish Year Book*, ed. Morris Fine and Milton Himmelfarb (Philadelphia: Jewish Publication Society, 1965 and 1968).

"Changing Social Characteristics of Orthodox, Conservative, and Reform Jews," *Sociological Analysis* 27 (Winter 1966): 210–22.

"Religion, Class, and Culture in American Jewish History," *The Jewish Journal of Sociology* 9, no. 2 (December 1967): 227–41.

TO CAROL

Your latest deed of loyalty is greater than the first
—Ruth 3:10

PREFACE

The American Jew is torn between two sets of values—those of integration and acceptance into American society and those of Jewish group survival. These values appear to me to be incompatible. But most American Jews do not view them in this way. The thesis of this book is that the behavior of the American Jew is best understood as his unconscious effort to restructure his environment and reorient his own self-definition and perception of reality so as to reduce the tension between these values.

Some observers of American Jewish behavior see the development of American Judaism as the adaptation of Judaism to the American environment. This oversimplifies the process. Jews respond both to the American environment and to their own tradition, a tradition, by the way, that was in the process of being reshaped when mass immigration to the United States took place toward the end of the last century. In the process of their response, American Jews in turn reshaped, with a remarkable degree of success, both their tradition and their environment.

The book is divided into three parts. Part one depicts the evolution of American Judaism from its European roots. It develops the basic theme of the book, stressing how the efforts to overcome the integration-survival tension led to particular conceptions of reality and, most importantly, to the redefinition by Jews of themselves as a "religion." Of course, it also led to particular forms of religious behavior and to a unique conception of Israel. Israel, as we will suggest in the final chapter of part one, provides the major symbolic content for the American Jewish religion today.

Part two illustrates the theme by focusing on special segments of the community—rabbis, youth, and radical college students—and on Jewish political liberalism, the great effort of American Jews to reshape their political environment to minimize the survival-integration tension.

Part three is a concluding chapter, with some thoughts on the future of Judaism in America.

My own position, which receives little expression in the book, is that if the Jewish community is to survive, it must become more explicit and conscious about the incompatibility of integration and survival. To do so today will offer the possibility for conscious choice. To refuse to do so will mean the continuing redefinition of Judaism, to the point where its existence is meaningless in any traditional sense. I have no doubt that some nominal form of Judaism will persist in the United States. However, the fact that some group, no matter how small, will continue to call itself Jewish, sharing some vague sense of history with a Jewish past and some pride in the unique contribution that this people has made to the world, offers me little consolation; nor will such a group in the last analysis be very helpful to American society. I want to see the perpetuation of the best of traditional Judaism. I would not be satisfied with a Quaker-like future for American Judaism, regardless of how sympathetic I may be to the ideals and contributions of the Quakers. But if Judaism as I understand it is to perpetuate itself in America, it must, at least to some extent, reject the value of integration, which I see as sapping its very essence.

* * *

I am indebted to a number of people who helped me in the formulation of my ideas. To three people, however, I owe a special debt. It is customary for an author to absolve those who were most helpful to him from the author's own errors of fact or opinion. In the case of Marshall Sklare that is easily done, since he has never read the manuscript. However, many of my ideas are derived from Sklare's publications and from my discussions with him when we taught at Yeshiva University. To Milton Himmelfarb I also owe special thanks. Himmelfarb read this manuscript in its entirety; but my debt to him far exceeds the helpful comments he made on this work. Many of my ideas are outgrowths of his *Commentary* articles and of my discussions with him. Beyond this, however, he edited three articles of mine in the *American Jewish Year Book* which inform this volume as well. The fact that I can reread those articles today without a sense of embarrassment is due entirely to his demanding and penetrating editorial standards. Since he refused to let me thank him in the *American Jewish Year Book* for what he considered an editor's normal responsibility, I welcome the opportunity to thank him here. Himmelfarb is a special kind of Jew. He carries his Judaism like a chip on his shoulder. The fact that no one has yet succeeded in knocking the chip off, and few dare even try, has served not only as a source of intellectual satisfaction but of religious inspiration to some, including myself.

Finally, my wife, Carol Liebman, to whom this book is dedicated, deserves more thanks than words can express for help with this manuscript and everything else I have done. She has meant so much to me—intellectually, emotionally, and spiritually—that I find it awkward even to attempt an expression of gratitude. I can only say that my politics, my religion, and my family are all due to her.

CONTENTS

The Ambivalent American Jew

PART ONE

The Jewish Tradition
in Its American
Formulation

1

RELIGION AND COMMUNALISM

If we want to understand Jewish life in America, we must
begin with traditional Judaism. In our own nontraditional secular terminology, traditional Judaism is best defined as a folk or
ethnic religion; but even this term may understate the interrelationship between religion and all other aspects of traditional
Jewish life.

Students of religion have distinguished basic religious structures; one such structure differentiates between religions that
are confined historically to a single people, that is, *folk religions,* and those which have spread among many people, that
is, *universal religions.* In folk religion, the community itself is
the carrier of the religion. A vital relationship exists between
the community as a whole and its God or gods. The content of
the folk religion delineates the peculiarity of the particular folk
involved[1] and extends the boundaries of religious concern to
the total life pattern of the community. Of course, in the process of religious institutionalization and organization (that is, as
the religious experience becomes objectified in a human institution and develops a specialized hierarchy of administrators,
priests, and clergy with their own self-interest in organizational
survival), certain changes in the universal or folk content of
each religion take place.

As man develops an increasing self-awareness and begins to rationalize his life independently of his folk or community, either through internal social and economic changes within the folk community or because of an external challenge which may destroy the basis of folk ties, the folk member is attuned to a religious message which speaks to his personal condition. Such a message may also appeal to other individuals in cultures outside the original group. Thus by cutting across several folk communities the religious message may become more universalized. Universal religion, on the other hand, develops its own community or church in the course of becoming institutionalized. Regardless of its ultimate goals, many characteristics of such a church community may come to resemble a folk community. In addition, a universal religion encounters folk communities as it spreads its message, and in each area it often takes on the peculiar stamp of the community in which it has been accepted.

There are other factors which tend to diminish the radical differences between folk religion and universal religion in their ideal-typical structure. Organized religion may represent objectification and institutionalization, reenactment and restructuring of a religious experience, but its basis still lies in a subjective experience and a need to relate to the "totally other" or to the "beyond." It represents man's effort to break through the constraints which are part of the routine of his life. Regardless of how intimately man is involved in his folk community, regardless of the degree to which religion is a shared experience related to the total life pattern of the community, its basis remains in personal experience. Fritz Kunkel has written: "Every woman who bears a child, every man who risks his life, every human being who dies, must pass through the utmost extremity without the help of his fellow creatures who are willing to assist him."[2]

Even folk religion contains within it the seeds of individual self-awareness. On the other hand, no matter how personal a universal religion may be, no matter how indifferent it is in theory to ties of family, kin, community, or nation, it arises within a community rooted in time and place, and it appeals to individuals who are part of other temporal and spatial communities. Universal religion therefore inevitably bears the stamp of the folk consciousness or mores out of which it sprang and to whom its initial appeal was addressed.

Some care has been taken in distinguishing between basic structures of religion, but it has also been noted that as universal religion and folk religion work themselves out, many of their differences fade. Nevertheless, the basic characteristic of either folk or universal religion is impressed on any particular religious group. Thus traditional Judaism contained universal elements from its very inception, but in contrast to Christianity it bears the mark of a basically folk religion. A few of these elements will be mentioned here.

Judaism considers its basis to lie in a covenant, the set of laws and practices commanded by God and accepted by the total Jewish community at a historic moment. Earlier covenants were concluded between God and the patriarchs (Abraham, Isaac, and Jacob) in which God bound Himself to the patriarchs' descendants. The major covenant was at Mount Sinai, however, where through Moses, God revealed His law to the total community. A Jew is born into the community and is therefore bound by the earlier covenants, just as God is bound to him. Thus by virtue of his birth, a Jew is always a Jew. He may be a bad Jew. He may even cease to identify himself as a Jew. But juridically he is still Jewish. Deviant behavior on his part may affect his status within Jewish law. He may be denied certain rights, his testimony in a Jewish court may be invalid, other Jews may be required to spurn or avoid him altogether, but he is still a Jew under religious law.

This is why, in the celebrated Brother Daniel case, the State of Israel found it was simply too awkward to adjudicate status under religious law. A Jew who was born Oswald Rufeisen converted to Catholicism and joined the Carmelite order as Brother Daniel. He joined that particular order because it had a monastery in Israel. Brother Daniel applied for Israeli citizenship under the Law of Return, which permits every Jewish immigrant to become a citizen of the country as soon as he sets foot on its soil.[3] He also asked to be listed as a Jew in the space on his identity card which provides for ethnic affiliation. The Ministry of the Interior decided that although Rufeisen could become a citizen through naturalization, he was not eligible for citizenship on the basis of the Law of Return. The ministry maintained that only a person who declares himself a Jew and does not belong to any other religion should be considered a Jew. The Supreme Court of Israel, in a four-to-one decision, upheld the Ministry of the Interior, but it declared that in refusing to classify a Catholic monk as a Jew, the court was applying secular law, not the religious law of Judaism.

Judaism does accept proselytes; that is, one can convert to Judaism. Like all other Jews, a proselyte invokes the patriarchs as his fathers. The use of the term father is not simply rhetorical. The concept of Jews as lineal descendants of Abraham, Isaac, and Jacob is of enormous importance in the essentially legalistic and textual Jewish tradition, since the covenantal community is based on ethnic and familial ties. Indeed, the Jewish nation was commanded to maintain special relationships with certain other nations, based on their descent from kin of the patriarchs. But how can a proselyte use the term father when he refers to Abraham, Isaac, or Jacob? The answer is that Jewish law denies the validity of any blood ties which the proselyte had prior to his conversion. Should his parents die, the proselyte need not observe the carefully prescribed laws of mourning incumbent on a bereaved child, for his blood relationships cease to have status in Jewish law. This occurs even when both parents and children become converts. Jews are known by the name of their parents. For example, one is called "Aaron the son of David." The proselyte assumes a new name, as the son or daughter of the patriarch Abraham, the first Jew. Thus a change in what we today might call religious status is a change in ethnic status as well. It is significant that when Ruth refused to leave Naomi, she expressed her desire with the words "Your people shall be my people, and your God my God."[4]

Labeling Judaism as any kind of religion involves a measure of arbitrariness. There is no early Jewish term for religion. The Hebrew equivalent, *dat*, was borrowed from the Persians and connotes law. Judaism never distinguished its religious dimension from its ethnic, national, folk, and cultural dimensions. These were intertwined and inseparable. Indeed, many of the premodern states treated Jews not only as a separate religion but almost as a foreign nationality, a separate body with legal autonomy and subject to its own leaders. It is only in the modern period, the emancipation period or just before it, that the problem of self-definition and the specification of Judaism as a religion, a culture, or a nationality arises.

The modern period has witnessed the breakdown of traditional Judaism.[5] Dating this period in Jewish life, however, is subject to some dispute; it is less a matter of objective fact than of historical theory. Broadly speaking, one may adopt either a sociointellectual approach or a sociopolitical interpretation. Taking the first approach, for example, one may date the modern period from the emergence of a religiously neutral society in the mid-eighteenth century. Alternately, one may date it from "the elevation of secular learning to an independent cultural value (e.g., Jewish girls studying French and music)."[6] Finally, one's criteria of modernity might be the beginning of skepticism and free thinking, which pushes its origins still further back.

In all these cases modernity is synonymous with Enlightenment and finds its clearest expression in intellectual currents. Enlightenment, however, was for Jews far more than an intellectual movement. It suggested the possibility of a truly open society in which anti-Semitism would be unknown and Jews virtually indistinguishable from non-Jews. What Ernst Cassirer says of the eighteenth-century Enlightenment was particularly true for Jews. Reason, he says, was understood

not as a sound body of knowledge, principles and truths, but as a kind of energy, a force which is fully comprehensible only in its agency and effects. . . . Its most important function consists in its power to bind and to dissolve. It dissolves everything merely factual, all simple data of experience, and everything believed on the evidence of revelation, tradition and authority.[7]

What magnificent promise such a movement must have for those Jews who believed that their own disabilities stemmed from the irrational and autocratic elements embedded in the traditions of Gentiles and the customs of Jews.

The period of Enlightenment and emancipation marked a turning point in modern Jewish history. The Jew admired the culture of the non-Jew, adopted the values of the Enlightenment, and judged himself and his institutions by non-Jewish standards. This was not the first time that Jews had initiated such reevaluation. For instance, it occurred during the Hellenistic period in both Alexandria and Palestine and in medieval Spain. In fact, the impact of the nineteenth-century Enlightenment was probably less severe and its reorientation of Jewish values less radical than that of Hellenism in the third and second centuries before the Common Era. But European Jews in the eighteenth and nineteenth centuries had no memories of that experience. As far as traditionalists were concerned, it would have been no more comforting to know about this past history than for frightened Americans in the late 1960s to be reminded that this country had survived Civil War riots and Shays's Rebellion.

The basic changes experienced by Judaism in this modern period were quickened and their impact diffused by their coincidence with political emancipation and the sense that political equality was based on the acceptance of new values. But the very intensity with which the Jewish community sought social and political equality was itself a reflection of its new values. Not the least important aspect of equality was the opportunity it brought the individual Jew to free himself from the compulsion of the Jewish community, giving him access to civil courts—his civil actions had heretofore been decided by Jewish courts—and freeing him from compulsion in matters of religious behavior.

Thus the full impact of the Enlightenment only occurred with the political emancipation of the Jews. The Enlightenment preceded emancipation among certain intellectual and economic classes of Jewish society,[8] and it prepared the way for the acceptance of emancipation. But it was emancipation which provided the political conditions which undercut the authority of traditional Judaism. Thus, although the granting of political rights to Jews may appear as a discrete act at a particular moment in time, it can only be understood as part of an evolutionary process. Furthermore, it occurred at different periods in various parts of Europe.

The struggle for emancipation of West European Jewry in England, France, and Germany took place roughly between 1780 and 1850.[9] The political emancipation of Central European Jewry (the Hungarian portion of the Hapsburg Empire) can be dated roughly as occurring between 1850 and 1880.[10] Emancipation in East Europe (Russia, pre-Congress Poland, and the modern states carved out of these territories) came about between around 1850 and the end of World War I.[11] As rough and approximate as these dates are, they must be further qualified. The early struggle for emancipation in the West had repercussions on the thinking of Jews in the East even before their own political status was secured. Furthermore, none of the terminal dates was really final because even after emancipation many Jewish communities were threatened by the loss of their political rights. As events between the two world wars were to prove, Jewish fears were not without substance.

However, traditional Judaism had already lost its meaning to upper-middle-class secularly educated Jews in the eighteenth century. The disintegration of the tradition proceeded at a rapid pace in Western Europe, extending to other classes of the Jewish population in the nineteenth century. At first, the decline of traditional Judaism was reflected in political and social rather than in spiritual aspects of the Jews' lives. It did not even involve a loss of faith in such fundamentalistic dogmas as the revelation of the Torah (the Pentateuch) by God to Moses. Rather, the breakdown of tradition was reflected in new Jewish aspirations for political rights and for acceptance by the non-Jew, and in a new hierarchy of values. Standards determining right and wrong or good and bad now became those of the gentile society. The political dimension of this change was the loss of confidence in the traditional lay and rabbinical leaders of the community. The nontraditionalists now sought to capture the leadership of the Jewish community or to escape its juridical arm. They sought acceptance by the gentile society, not because of their Jewishness, not despite their Jewishness, but because their Jewishness was irrelevant.

All these efforts, both social and political, necessitated a self-definition whereby the character of the new Jew could be identified, and if necessary the differences between the traditionalist Jew and the nontraditionalist Jew could be clarified, so that at least the latter might obtain the rights and privileges he sought.

The formation of new nation-states also raised problems of definition. Were the Jews to be granted political equality? Were they a foreign element unassimilable into the new nation-state, or were they only different from other citizens in form but not in kind? The question could only be answered by defining the nature of Judaism; in its solution lay the answer of whether Jews could or could not be granted political equality. Thus we find in the emancipation period the convergence of forces both internal and external to the Jewish community pressing for a definition of Judaism.

The new nontraditional Jew sought political and social equality. The first step was the achievement of political rights. These rights in turn depended upon the state's definition of Judaism and Jews. The question posed was, in essence, whether Judaism was a national-cultural-ethnic community similar to other minority groups in Eastern and Central Europe, or whether it was a religious minority similar to religious groups in Western Europe.

From the vantage point of the twentieth century it appears that choosing either alternative at the expense of the other involved a deviation from the essence of the tradition. The alternatives which Jews actually chose were influenced by the prevailing ideas within each nation-state as to what was or was not acceptable as a condition for political emancipation.

Essentially, Jews in Western Europe—France, England, and Germany—chose the religious option. The enlightened Jews of the middle and upper classes redefined themselves as a religion and called themselves Frenchmen or Germans of the Mosaic faith. These radicals, the Reform Jews, then sought to reform the Jewish religion in harmony with prevailing values of rationalism and universalism, which had not yet given way to nineteenth-century romanticism when the new Judaism of Western Europe was formulated.

Within two or three generations the traditionalists disappeared entirely in Western Europe. In their place Orthodox Jews emerged. These were Jews who refused to compromise the religious aspects of their tradition, arguing that such compromises were unnecessary, since Judaism was already in harmony with the best philosophical thought of the age, and accepting the new definition of Judaism as a religion. Where Orthodoxy was a vital force, as in Germany, the internal Jewish conflict was a religious one between Orthodox and Reform. For many wealthy and secularly educated Jews this conflict was of little moment. Even Reform, to say nothing of Orthodoxy, was too parochial and too trapped in an increasingly outmoded terminology of eighteenth-century rationalism to have much appeal. But we are not concerned with Jews who left the fold entirely, for their impact on evolving forms of Jewish life, particularly in America, where this conflict continued, was negligible.

Of course, the transformation proceeded in spurts rather than smoothly or suddenly. It would be a vulgarization of Jewish intellectual history to suggest that the ideologists of either Reform or Orthodoxy, with one eye on the values of gentile society, simply overhauled traditional Judaism. It would be more proper to suggest a certain "elective affinity," to borrow Max Weber's terminology, between the desire for emancipation and social equality on the part of many Jews, and certain notions about the nature of Judaism which were current from the late eighteenth century to the middle of the nineteenth century.

The situation in Eastern and Central Europe was more complex. Nationalism arrived later there, complicated by the existence of territorial or linguistic minorities, or both, each of which felt attachments to different nation-states. Thus there were Slovaks, Poles, and Ukrainians, to mention only a few groups within the Hungarian portion of the Austro-Hungarian Empire, and Germans in Poland. Nationalism had to come to terms with these national, cultural, and territorial minorities, and the addition of a Jewish national or cultural minority was a problem not very different in kind. Many of these other minorities had their own national churches anyway, which further reinforced their feeling of distinctiveness. This gave some impetus to a definition of Judaism along national-cultural lines, with religion incidental to national culture. This situation stood in contrast to Western Europe, where the sharpest religious conflict was between clericalist and anticlericalist and, instead of coinciding with linguistic and cultural polarization, was often fought along class lines.

In addition, the Jewish minority of Eastern and Central Europe reacted quite differently to the dominant national culture from the way the Jews of Western Europe did. Among the latter, German or French culture offered a standard worthy of assimilation. The Jew often felt a sense of inferiority and personal worthlessness when he was confronted by the traditions and cultural achievements of France and Germany. This was less true of Russia, Poland, and Hungary, and even less so of Slovakia, Lithuania, and Latvia. Therefore, it is not surprising that, on one hand, Jewish traditionalists retained their identity much longer in Eastern Europe, where external pressure for redefinition was less intense and specific in its direction, and that, on the other hand, those who broke from traditional Judaism chose the cultural-national rather than the religious option.

The national or cultural definition in turn subsumed a variety of forms: Jewish socialism, Zionism, cultural autonomy. But, as Salo W. Baron has written, "whether or not they hoped to become some day a political nationality, in the stricter sense, by erecting a state of their own, most East European Jews now began asserting that their national culture was distinct from that of all other cultural and linguistic groups."[12] Although some of these Jews were desirous of religious reform, Reform Judaism as a religious movement made little headway. Religion was either irrelevant or a matter of secondary concern to the nontraditionalists. The conflict among East European Jews was articulated in political, social, and economic, rather than religious, terms. Thus, paradoxically, the theoretical basis for a modus vivendi between the traditionalists and many nontraditionalists existed in Eastern Europe, where none existed in the West. As long as the nontraditionalist Jew did not challenge the religious authority or legitimacy of the traditionalist, accommodations could be made. Many nontraditionalists desired this accommodation because consciously or unconsciously many aspects of traditional Judaism formed a cultural basis and served to legitimize new communal structures whose evolution they anticipated. The Zionists, for example, who asserted a nationalist definition of Judaism, refused to accept converts to another faith as members, although they "received with open arms Jews having no religious affiliation."[13]

Severe conflict between traditionalists and Zionists developed only when the Zionists' redefinition of Judaism required the establishment of cultural alternatives to traditional Judaism. The indifference of traditionalists to political Zionism changed to open hostility when the Zionists approved a program for their own schools. But because the Jewish identity of the traditionalists included broad cultural and national aspects, they were reluctant to split themselves off from the new increasingly voluntaristic Jewish community. In Germany, Orthodox and Reform established their own communities. But in Poland, traditionalists, Zionists, and Socialists vied for control of one community. Jewish self-definition in East Europe resulted naturally in the establishment of a number of Jewish political parties. In Western Europe such parties would have been unthinkable.

The distinction between the two Jewries, Eastern and Western, is nicely illustrated in the battle that took place in 1937 within Agudat Israel over its policies toward the establishment of a Jewish state.[14] Agudat Israel was the major international organization which united traditionalists of the East and the Orthodox of the West in the period between the world wars. It was militantly anti-Zionist. The chief topic of debate at its 1937 convention was whether it should endorse the Peel Commission report of the British government; this report recommended a division of Palestine between Jews and Arabs and the creation of two independent territorial units. The religious arguments against endorsing the Peel Commission report were weighty. A portion of the land which Jews believed to be invested with sanctity, which was promised by God to the Jewish people, was to be surrendered to the Arabs. At the political level there was opposition to a Jewish state, which everyone feared would be controlled by Zionists and secularists.

Nevertheless, the leading rabbis and delegates from Eastern Europe urged endorsement of the Peel Commission report. The traditionalist masses of Eastern Europe no less than the Zionists, the rabbinical elite no less than the poor ignorant Jews, were faithful to the millennial Jewish hope for a return to Zion. Partisan religious considerations and definitions gave way before the traditional sense of a united peoplehood and the hope for a concrete resolution of communal problems. It was the Orthodox of Western Europe who opposed the Peel Commission report and most bitterly opposed practical steps toward establishing a Jewish state, thereby ignoring their national-cultural tradition. (This situation represented a reversal of positions adopted some thirty years before. At that time the Zionists of Eastern Europe, despite their aspiration for a national political state, had rejected the British offer of Uganda as a national homeland, insisting instead on Palestine as the only home of the Jewish people, consonant with their religious tradition. It was the secularist Zionists of Western Europe who first considered accepting the British offer of Uganda, thereby ignoring their religious tradition.) Jewish self-definition in Eastern Europe, whether secular or traditional, was rooted in culture and community. In Western Europe it was rooted in religion whose community was only a by-product.

Certain aspects of the Central European resolution should be considered separately. By the middle of the nineteenth century the Austro-Hungarian Empire was the home of many nationality groups, all striving for some degree of autonomy or self-determination. But the self-definition of each group and the territorial boundaries they claimed for themselves by no means complemented one another. For example, Hungarian nationalists, with their Magyar culture, sought independence from Austria but subsumed Slovakia within their territorial homeland. The Slovaks, in turn, who constituted a linguistic and

territorial minority within Hungary, sought their own indepen-
cence.

Given the number of minority groups within the Austro-
Hungarian Empire, the Jews might have been expected to
define themselves culturally or nationally, as they did in Eastern Europe, rather than religiously, as in Western Europe. But
this did not occur. Nowhere were the Jewish people more
sharply divided than in Hungary. The split was between Orthodox and Neolog (religious reformers), not between traditionalists and secularists. Furthermore, in Hungary, as in Western
Europe, intermarriage and assimilation had reached high pro-
portions by the end of the nineteenth century and the beginning of the twentieth. This phenomenon was characteristic of
Jewish societies with a religious rather than a communal self-
definition. If Judaism is basically a religion like Christianity,
then presumably one would cease to identify oneself as a Jew
once one no longer believed in the religion or practiced it. But
if Judaism is a community based on ethnicity, culture, and
family, then one cannot very well opt out. The question then
becomes: Why did the Jews of Hungary adopt a religious self-
definition? The answer may lie in the implied price the Jews
had to pay for emancipation.

In Hungary, the Magyars were the dominant group politically and socioeconomically. From their point of view, the
minority problem in Hungary was their own numerical weakness. Hence they sought the alliance of those "foreign elements
who were willing to identify themselves with and assimilate
into the Magyar nation."[15] Proponents of Jewish emancipation
argued that the Jews were the most likely candidates for assimilation, because they already exhibited tendencies to adopt the
Hungarian language and culture. Some argued, further, that if
the Christians rectified the wrongs committed against Jews, the
Jews would be drawn to Christianity. Many opponents of emancipation did not necessarily oppose Jewish equality as such, "but
rather wished to tie it to certain conditions, particularly reli-

gious reforms, which would abolish those features of the Jewish religion that hinder social integration."[16] Those who absolutely opposed emancipation argued that there were too many Jews; consequently, the Magyars would not be able to assimilate them into their national values. But the Jewish search for allies in Hungary led to a religious, rather than a national-cultural, self-definition.

After Hungary achieved a measure of autonomy within the Austro-Hungarian Empire it granted emancipation to the Jews. In areas where the land was inhabited by non-Magyar nationalities, such as Transylvania, Hungarian national policy (beginning with the census of 1880) insisted that Jews be classified as Hungarian nationals.

A comparison of Jews in Hungary and those in Czechoslovakia will be most instructive. Up to this point one can note not only conceptual but also historical relevance to American Jewry. Those Jews whom we have discussed came to the United States with their particular conceptions of Judaism already formed. Czechoslovakia was a creation of the post-World War I peace conference. Czech Jews did not come to the United States in large numbers. Nevertheless, the situation in Czechoslovakia demonstrates the influence of the social environment and of political "reasons of state" on the Jewish minority's conception of itself.

Czechoslovakia, like other countries of Central Europe, was a multinational and multilingual state. But the interests of the dominant nationality group, the Czechs, unlike those of the Hungarian Magyars, favored a national definition of Judaism.[17] In the part of Czechoslovakia known as the Historic Lands (Bohemia and Moravia), the largest minority groups were Germans and Poles. The Jewish community there had already developed historical attachments to German culture and language. Language was the basis upon which minority groups in Czechoslovakia were defined. By this criterion most Jews would have been included within the German minority. In order to avoid increasing the number of Germans, Czechoslovakia permitted the Jews to define themselves as a separate minority, regardless of their language. Indeed, they were encouraged to identify themselves as a separate nationality. If they had been defined only religiously and then permitted to choose between Czech and German nationality for census purposes, most of the Bohemian and Moravian Jews, at least during the early years of the republic, would have chosen the national group with whom they felt the greatest cultural affinity. If the Jews had been defined linguistically, like all other nationality groups, again most of them would have been classified as Germans.

Jews therefore were given the opportunity of choosing Jewish nationality. Their actual choice was often fraught with far-reaching consequences. Czechoslovakia was divided into judicial districts. Minorities had to constitute 20 percent of the population in any given district in order to be eligible for such minority rights as publicly supported schools in their own language. In one Moravian district Germans constituted 19.71 percent of the population. The addition of German-speaking Jews would have given them far more than the 20 percent they needed. The Germans insisted that, since the basis of minority definition was language, the Jews be included in their total. But the Czechoslovakian courts ruled that those Jews who claimed Jewish nationality had to be counted separately from the Germans, regardless of their language.[18]

In view of the minority situation in Czechoslovakia, it is not surprising that many leaders of the republic were outspoken friends of the Zionist movement. But recalling the period with which we are dealing, we see that a new factor of Jewish self-definition became relevant. The Jews of Bohemia and Moravia had already been shaped by the forces of Enlightenment and emancipation before Czechoslovakia became an independent state. The critical moment in Jewish history when major values were subject to radical reformulation had passed. Jews of the Historic Lands had already arrived at a self-definition in which religion, rather than nationality, was stressed. Nevertheless, the environmental impact was not to be denied.

The Jews of Bohemia and Moravia were liberal rather than Orthodox in religious practice, a pattern already set by their earlier orientation toward the West. Nevertheless, "in all of Czechoslovakia there was no organized movement of Liberal Judaism comparable to the one in Germany, which systematically promoted the practice and ideology of Liberal religion."[19] Rather, as in Eastern Europe, the fight was between varying interpretations of Jewish communalism.

Under pressure of Czech nationalism, German-speaking Jewish assimilationists intensified their identification with Judaism, and even supported the cultural aspirations of the Zionists. Where they refused, the Czech government lent its support to the nationalists or communalists within the community. In 1920 Czech Jewish assimilationists in Moravia objected to the Jewish Religious Congregations (the representative body of Jews in Czechoslovakia) engaging in social and cultural activities in behalf of Palestine. Their petition reached the authorities of the Czechoslovak Republic, who felt that the matter must be left to the religious leaders of the congregations. The Rabbinical Associations of Bohemia and Moravia maintained that "social and cultural activities were to be considered integral parts of the Jewish religion,"[20] and it was this opinion that was accepted as authoritative by the Czech government.

In other sections of Czechoslovakia, Slovakia, and Ruthenia, the masses of Jews were East European in culture and orientation. Here the conflict was between traditionalists and secular communalists. Reform Judaism was quite weak. There was a Jewish political party organized to secure parliamentary representation for Jews in Czechoslovakia. This party was opposed by the traditionalists of Slovakia, who organized their own party and benefited from financial contributions by the Agrarian party, who thereby sought to divert votes away from the major Jewish party. In Ruthenia, which was the most agrarian and traditionalist of all the Czech provinces, the divisions among Jews were entirely between the Zionists and the religious traditionalists.

At this point it may be helpful to summarize our discussions.

1. Traditional Judaism was a religious civilization. It made no distinction between ethnicity, nationality, culture, and religion. The particular characteristics delineating each of these concepts—ethnicity-family; nationality-territory; culture: language, literature, and art; and religion: beliefs about ultimate reality, the nature of man, and the need to communicate with the "totally other"—were all intertwined and interrelated. The family was the foundation for Jewish life, and religious ceremony revolved primarily about the home. Territorially, although Jews lived outside the land of Israel, they were painfully conscious of the fact. Symbols within the home as well as the liturgy and many rituals reminded the Jew of the destruction of the Temple and his present condition of exile. Cultural life was also organized around religious symbols and ceremonies. During the medieval Spanish period Jews had written poems of satire and romance, and even drinking songs. But the historical memory of Judaism retained only those literary creations which had religious or communal significance. Nothing illustrates this point so well as the inclusion of the Song of Songs in the biblical canon precisely because the Jewish people were able to read this as a love song between God and Israel.

2. Traditional Judaism declined in the period of Enlightenment and emancipation. A new Jew arose to whom the interrelationships of ethnicity, nationality, culture, and religion had lost resonance. The religious symbols no longer evoked the memories, the longings, and the hopes they once did. Jewish values lost their authority. The individual Jew and eventually the entire Jewish community increasingly oriented themselves toward achieving a new position and status within gentile society.

3. These new stirrings within the Jewish community coincided in Europe with new secular conceptions of the nation-state and the autonomy of national interests.

4. The forces both within the Jewish community and outside of it led to redefinitions of Judaism in which one aspect of Judaism was stressed at the expense of the other. Which aspect received the most emphasis was determined by the larger society's concept of legitimacy. In Western Europe, religion was stressed, and the natural-cultural-communal aspects of the tradition were de-emphasized, reformulated, or simply denied. In Eastern Europe, traditionalists maintained a stronghold. Those who broke from the tradition found their identity in the secularization of the national-cultural-communal aspects of the tradition.

The interaction between the environment and forces within Judaism in shaping Jewish self-definition has been stressed. The foregoing should not suggest that Jewish self-consciousness was totally dependent on its environment. The interaction or mutual influence is present first of all in the particular form taken by religious or communal self-definition. Furthermore, as happened in Czechoslovakia, once Jewish self-definition was shaped on the crucible of the Enlightenment and emancipation it became less malleable to social and political forces in the larger society. It would seem, however, that in the period in which Jews broke with their traditional past they were particularly susceptible to new formulations and conceptions in accordance with the social and political conditions of the larger society. This is precisely the situation which many North African and Yemenite Jews are experiencing in Israel today.

5. The basic options of European Jewry were religious, or what we have called communal. Where Jews chose the religious option, as in Western Europe, we find Reform Judaism, a high rate of intermarriage and assimilation, de-emphasis of the Hebrew language, anti-Zionism on the part of the leaders of the community, and an Orthodox religious group which favored

secular education and participated in the social and political life of the country, but separated itself from the non-Orthodox Jews. In those countries where the communal option was chosen, we find Jewish political parties, a demand for cultural separation, strong Zionist orientation among the masses, an absence of religious Reform, low rates of intermarriage and assimilation, and a traditional Judaism which opposed secular education and did not encourage participation in the social and political life of the country, but remained part of the total Jewish community vying for its leadership.

2

INTEGRATION AND SURVIVAL

Jewish identity in the preemancipation period assumed essentially one of two forms—religion or communalism. Each in its own way was a break with tradition. Each was predicated on acceptance of the surrounding society's values and a desire for acceptance by the surrounding society. But whether Jews or Jewish communities chose the religious or the communal option, they were not only responding to or internalizing values from without. Both the religious and communal options had roots within traditional Judaism. More important, both were not only strategies of acceptance, but also strategies of Jewish survival. We must never forget, therefore, that if survival values had been absent from the Jewish community, it would have simply disappeared.

Then, as today, the majority of Jews were torn between two forces: the desire for acceptance by the gentile society and the attraction of non-Jewish values and attitudes, and the desire for group identity and survival as a distinct community. This phenomenon is, of course, not unique to Jews, but the intensity of both forces is probably more pronounced among the Jews than in any other group in American society. The Italian immigrants, for example, resisted acculturation more strenuously than did the Jews, but their second and third generations are barely distinguishable as a separate group. Even the Irish, despite their reputation as a proud, defiant, separate subgroup in American society, are not only disappearing rapidly but seem to take pride in their loss of identity. The Amish, however, are far more resistant to acculturation than are the Jews. But the Amish do not insist that, concurrently with their separatism, American society close its eyes to their distinctiveness in economic, political, and social considerations.

Not so the Jews. In addition to their desire to be treated as equals, they demand that their Jewishness cease to be a factor in any judgment which society exercises over them. Jews, for example, do not argue that since they comprise a certain percentage of New York City's population they are entitled to a similar percentage of the political offices. On the contrary, they argue that their Jewishness should simply be irrelevant to such considerations. Yet Jews are quite conscious of their proportion of officeholders, college presidents, and large corporation directors. Where the number of Jews is less than might be anticipated, they suspect that discrimination is involved.

Most Jews oppose intermarriage. Jewish parents will raise strong objections if their son informs them that he is marrying a non-Jewish girl. But if the son adds that his girl friend's parents also object to the marriage, the Jewish parents will either be outraged by their "anti-Semitism" or else fail to understand what basis they have for raising objections.

Jews do not argue that equality means that public support for education should include public support for Jewish schools. Rather, many argue that public support for education should not be extended to any nonpublic school. (The very existence of Jewish schools is an acute source of embarrassment to many Jews.)

Jews incessantly demand that they be treated as though Jewishness does not exist. Nothing pleases most Jews more than to be told that they don't look Jewish or behave Jewishly, that they cannot be distinguished in their appearance, dress, speech, attitudes, or behavior from the non-Jew.

While this is all true, Jews still want to be Jews. They don't flock to Christian ministers for conversion. They don't even flock to the Unitarian Universalist church or to the Ethical Culture Society. The latter, a nontheist religion established by Jews who didn't want Christianity but found Judaism too parochial, has never attracted large numbers of Jews. Classical Reform Judaism and temples such as New York City's Temple Emanu-El are more characteristic institutions of assimilated Jews. The temples of classical Reform Judaism, particularly at the turn of the century, were barely distinguishable from liberal Christian churches.[1] One Protestant is reported to have wandered into Temple Emanu-El and only discovered by chance that he was in a Jewish synagogue. But there is a difference—the name. And that is how Jews seem to want it.

Jews want full acceptance as Americans, not as Jews. But they are scandalized by intermarriage, insist that a non-Jewish partner in a marriage convert to Judaism even when, as is usually the case, that partner no longer considers himself (generally herself) Christian. They support the State of Israel financially, politically, and emotionally when such support must surely raise the specter of dual national loyalty, if not outright disloyalty to America; but they are outraged by the idea that the State Department discriminates against Jews in its personnel policies.

The representative Jew, wherever he stands on a survival-integration continuum, is himself pulled in both directions. It is as an individual that he feels the severest tension in this basic dilemma, with the result that no position at either extreme of the continuum finds exposition or even tolerance among most Jews. The extreme survival position is represented by some Hasidic groups popularly labeled as ultra-Orthodox. Such groups tend to be indifferent to the rest of the American Jewish community and quite incapable of communicating with them. Another extreme survivalist position is represented by some

Zionist youth groups. Members of these groups either emigrate to Israel (where they often discover that they were more closely tied to American culture than they thought), or they reach adulthood and begin to conform to prevailing American Jewish patterns. Rebellious youth today is attracted by the slogan "Never trust anyone over thirty." The attitude of Zionist youth might be paraphrased as "Never trust a Zionist over thirty if he's still living in America." Significantly, many Hasidic groups have also found that only emigration to Israel can insure a steadfast devotion to survival.

It is difficult to find articulation of an extreme integration or assimilationist position. If one merely wants to be integrated into American society without any concern for group survival, the first sensible thing to do is to stop talking about it, which simply attracts attention. An organization which most Jews consider single-mindedly devoted to assimilation is the American Council for Judaism. This is unfair. If its members only wanted to be accepted by non-Jews, why would they organize a Jewish group? The American Council for Judaism does not simply want integration. It does stand charged with Jewish self-hatred and anti-Semitism. But in pursuing its goals it is willing to adopt positions which are deviant not only by Jewish but also by American standards. It was pro-Arab and anti-Israel during the last two decades, when the overwhelming majority of Americans were sympathetic to Israel. It denied the existence of Soviet anti-Semitism, which involved closing its eyes to facts and legitimizing the inhumane policies of America's arch-rival. Surely this is no way to promote its own acceptance.

An extreme survival position is incompatible with integration, just as an extreme integration position is incompatible with survival. Most Jews are not interested in the articulation of either position. On the contrary, the typical Jew is more anxious to find an ideological position which denies the existence of any tension between survival and integration. American Jews do this by blurring reality, obscuring the real referents for those concepts which they find most attractive. Jews do not believe in the congruence of American and Israeli policies because they have reflected upon the matter; nor do they believe in it as a strategy to justify their support for Israel in the eyes of the non-Jews. Rather, it is they themselves who require the rationale. Jews themselves must believe that American and Israeli interests are compatible, for otherwise they would be forced to make a choice between two values, each of which is desired.

Jewish organizations take public pride in the hyperactivism of many young Jews in movements for peace, civil rights, and social justice. They are disturbed only because such young people have very tenuous ties to Judaism. They maintain that the youths' social activism is an outcome of traditional Jewish values, even when the activists deny any relationship between what they are doing and Jewish values. Jewish spokesmen argue that if such Jews only knew what real Jewish values were, their identity would be strengthened. But the spokesmen themselves never articulate what they mean by Jewish values—it is very clear that they don't know. When pressed, they talk about civil rights, social justice, and peace. Trapped in the circularity of their arguments, they simply avoid discussion concerning the content of Jewish values. Since values are intrinsically rather than extrinsically desired, it is obvious that what such spokesmen call Jewish values are not values per se. They are, paradoxically, only the means to strengthen what the Jewish community really considers important: Jewish identity and communal survival.

The integration-survival alternatives, and the refusal of the majority of Jews to recognize them as alternatives or to choose between them, serve to define both the reality of the Jewish problem and the nature of the Jewish response. Three example problems amply illustrate this: anti-Semitism, Jewish-Negro relations, and the parochialism-humanism conflict.

ANTI-SEMITISM

The refusal of most American Jews to choose between integration and survival affects both their definition and their perception of anti-Semitism. Classical Zionism accepted anti-Semitism as a natural phenomenon—the hostility to outsiders or foreigners who, even when granted equal rights, were never accepted as equals. According to Theodor Herzl, emancipation only increased anti-Semitism because "the very impossibility of getting at the Jews nourishes and embitters hatred of them."[2] The only solution, therefore, was some form of Jewish autonomy. According to Chaim Weizmann, if there was one place where the Jews were not a minority and could therefore express themselves in their own way, "our relation to other races and nations would become more normal. We would not have to be always on the defensive or, on the contrary, become too aggressive, as always happens with a minority forced to be constantly on the defensive."[3]

Jews who desire integration can hardly accept the assumption that anti-Semitism is the outcome of hostility to strangers or foreigners. The Jew may admit that he is *treated* as a stranger or foreigner, but, unlike the classical Zionist, he does not begin by affirming that he *is* one. The question is: Why are Jews treated as strangers? The Zionist answers: "Because we are strangers." The typical American Jew would answer: "Because there is something wrong with those who treat us as strangers." American Jewish organizations respond to the anti-Semite by analyzing him psychologically ("an authoritarian personality") or sociologically ("downwardly mobile, creating imaginary enemies to account for his economic condition"). More popularly, he is considered either simply misinformed or an evil man.

Pure survivalists would agree that the anti-Semite is an evil man—but would add that it is his anti-Semitism which makes him evil, not some personality syndrome.

The pure survivalist is likely to accept a certain level of anti-

Semitism as unavoidable. He is likely to search for amelioration of its more serious manifestations in the Jewish condition or the Jewish situation or the behavior of Jews; he is far less concerned with the anti-Semite than with his behavior.

This already involves us in our second question—the perception of anti-Semitism. Although the impact of anti-Semitism on the quality of Jewish life in the past has been ambiguous, most Jews believe that it poses a threat to communal survival. This is curious, because there is no evidence that anti-Semitism, short of genocide, is such a threat. It may threaten the economic and social welfare of the Jews, but not their survival. In fact, Jewish life has often flourished in the face of outgroup hostility. But the assumption that anti-Semitism threatens survival is understandable if one also assumes that even under conditions of hostility Jews will retain the option of assimilation. The individual Jew then asks himself is he and his friends would choose to remain Jewish if this choice entailed severe economic and social hardship. A pure survivalist is likely to answer in the affirmative. Therefore, the many unfortunate consequences of anti-Semitism do not include, at least for him, a threat to Jewish survival. But for the overwhelming majority of American Jews, the answer to such a question is that Judaism is not worth the price of social and economic disabilities. In fact, once the Jew does suffer hardship as a result of anti-Semitism, he also finds that other things, including his own self-perception and the willingness of society to permit him to assimilate, do not remain constant. But when the problem is purely conjectural, it is perfectly understandable that to all except those at the survivalist end of the continuum, anti-Semitism poses a threat to survival.

Jewish student radicalism has been charged with having given rise to anti-Semitism. Chapter 8 will consider the phenomenon fully; here I shall discuss only the Jews' response to this accusation. One might argue that if anti-Semitism is the price Jews must pay for following their moral convictions, even at the cost of survival, Jews must be willing to pay it. Or one could argue that if student activism leads to anti-Semitism, the organized Jewish community must dissociate itself from the activities of student militants for its own protection. But either alternative involves a hard choice along the survival-integration continuum.

The integrationist might well risk the cost of anti-Semitism, assuming he acknowledged such a cost. This is currently the characteristic response of the most marginal elements of the Jewish community. They assume that integration means the freedom to respond to the environment solely as an individual, thereby denying or deeming irrelevant the possibility that the nature and content of one's response may itself be a function of one's Jewishness. Perhaps it is paradoxical to call this an integrationist response, since the content or direction of the students' activity—for example, sit-ins and militant demonstrations—is a deviation from American norms. One must remember, however, that from the Jew's point of view integration in American society is a structural, rather than an ideological, phenomenon. The test of integration is not what one does or says, but rather the channel or institution through which one participates in the society. A Jew who is also a Communist is integrated into American society despite his political deviance, because his participation occurs within an organization which is Jewishly neutral. The activity of student militants, therefore, no matter how deviant it may be, is structurally integrationist from a Jewish perspective. In contrast, Orthodox Jews who supported Lyndon Johnson's hawkish position on Vietnam were less integrated than student doves if they did so from a conviction that communism is a menace to Jews or that it is inappropriate for Jews to criticize any fundamental American policy not affecting Jews directly.

Those who stand closer to the survival end of the continuum are more likely to adopt the second alternative; they are most likely to dissociate the Jewish community from the activity of the student radicals—unless they happen to be particularly

committed to the students' values. This is unlikely because survivalists are more concerned with particularly Jewish problems
than with the structure of American universities and student
power. But they are most sensitive to the argument that the
student radicals must be more conscious of the impact of their
activity on the position of American Jews. The survivalists not
only thereby assert a proposition about the potential of Jews to
precipitate anti-Semitic responses from society, but they also
assert a belief about the nature of Jew-Gentile relations in the
United States. The survivalists assume that non-Jews perceive
Jews as having some quasi-corporate status and mutual responsibility. They feel that the Gentile believes that the Jew is not
in fact integrated into American society as an individual but
rather accepted as a member of a tolerated group.

An integrationist is likely to react to the assertion that student
radicalism leads to anti-Semitism with the response "So what?"
A survivalist is likely to favor steps which dissociate the Jewish
community from the radicals. But neither of these responses is
acceptable to the majority of Jews, torn between the two poles,
yet denying the very existence of the tension. Their characteristic response is to deny the validity of the assertion. This is
reflected in the reaction to a speech before the annual meeting
of the American Jewish Committee. The Anglo-Jewish press
reported:

> An editor of the New York Times called Columbia University today
> "The Peyton Place of Jewish Extremism" and cautioned that the eyes
> of the U.S. were upon it. He said it could lead to the kind of antisemit-
> ism now sweeping east European countries.
>
> Speaking to the 62nd annual meeting Harry Schwartz asserted that
> "Columbia's Jewish extremist students believe that anarchy and de-
> struction are useful for its own sake. They are trying to trample Co-
> lumbia and this is a tragedy for Judaism which has always had the
> highest regard for education."
>
> Although the most oppressive communists of the past were not Jews,
> he said, the "thousands of second line Jews who held important jobs

in communist regimes in Russia, Roumania, Poland and Hungary still linger vividly in European minds. They were the visible Jews and the people remember." Thus, Schwartz pointed bleakly to Columbia University where, he said, Jewish extremists there today could cause a similar situation in the future for American Jews.

At the conclusion of the address, former executive director John Slawson took the floor and denounced the talk, labelling it "the most disastrous" he has ever heard in his long career with the AJC. It was the antithesis of everything the AJC stands for, he declared.

AJC President Morris Abram told the *Post and Opinion:* "I do not agree with Schwartz."

Dr. Slawson later said privately that he held no brief for Columbia students but objected to the "Jewish" interpretation.[4]

Officials and the American Jewish Committee argued that if American Jews accepted the notion that what Jews *do* can cause anti-Semitism, they could not participate as full-fledged members of American society. Therefore, they argued, Jews must live by the myth (my term) that the content or direction of Jewish participation in American society, as long as it is done on an individual basis, can have no effect on anti-Semitism. Unlike the student activists, American Jewish Committee adherents are sensitive to the dangers of anti-Semitism and devote many of their resources to combatting it. But their integrative values lead them to deny the existence of Jewishly self-precipitating anti-Semitism unless the acitivity is itself organized through explicitly Jewish channels. For example, the American Jewish Committee has always been hypersensitive to the charges of a "Jewish vote" and has taken great pains to deny its existence. A "Jewish vote," they feel, could result in anti-Semitism precisely because such Jewish activity would have a group basis, which they eschew. But if they admitted that Jews, acting as individuals, can precipitate anti-Semitism, they would have to recognize the limits of integration; they would then be forced to choose between integration and survival. This is a choice they refuse to make.

JEWISH-NEGRO RELATIONS

The major contacts between Negroes and Jews during the past few decades occurred at about five points. Jews were highly visible to Negroes as retail merchants in Negro neighborhoods and to a lesser extent as owners of slum properties. With increasing ethnic consciousness, Jews also became visible as social workers and educators (teachers, principals, and other administrators). They were somewhat less visible in the latter two roles because the professional orientation of the occupations tended to blur their Jewish image. But as Negroes made increasingly specific and expressive demands from the school and welfare systems, they necessarily became conscious of the special or ascriptive characteristics of the individuals holding the professional roles within the system. In other words, black militancy has been accompanied by an ideology which denies the universality, and hence the professionalism, of what heretofore were accepted as general educational values.

The Negroes argue that such values are, in fact, particularistic in discriminating against the Negro. The charge of discrimination is leveled at both the application of the professional system —for example, the white middle-class content of the school curriculum—and the recruitment standards professional roles —the absence of Negroes as teachers, principals, and welfare workers, and the prevalence of Jews in these roles. The presence of large numbers of Jews is evidence to the Negro that the system is indeed particularistic in its operation. It not only excludes Negroes but also favors one other group in particular. Whether the Negro argument is true is not the issue here, only the fact that many Negroes believe it.

Another contact between Negroes and Jews was in the fight against legal discrimination, the traditional arena of civil rights. This brought the middle-class Negro and the Jew together. But with a decline in the emphasis on integration and fighting legal barriers and discrimination among northern Negroes, the one favorable contact has lost relevance and importance. Current contacts are sources of abrasion and conflict, such as Negro demands for white-collar employment in the public sector. Here again, the Negro, already sensitive to the Jewish presence, often finds a disproportionate number of Jews.

From the Jewish perspective at a grass-roots level, Jews are terrified by Negro violence and threats to their physical safety. For many, the image of the Negro as the "suffering servant" has changed to an image of one terrorizing for the sake of terror. The Negro is often viewed as the potential activist in new pogroms. But this image is not presently reflected in the organized Jewish community or among Jewish spokesmen.

It is interesting to note the issues to which leaders of Jewish organizations have responded. Both Negro demands to exclude white (Jewish) store owners from ghetto areas and the rioting, which is perceived by some as directed against Jews in particular, exacerbate the problem, although not as critically as in other areas of conflict. That is because it affects fewer outspoken Jews, particularly the more affluent, younger, or intellectual ones. The efforts of the Negro to secure more white-collar positions threaten the Jews who presently hold these positions, and this has been reflected in the statements of some Jewish spokesmen.

More critical for the organized Jewish community is the Negro challenge to professionalism. This goes to the very heart of Jewish accommodation to American society, an accommodation which involves the defense of universalism and achievement, as opposed to particularism and ascription. This accommodation insists that one's race, religion, or ethnic group is absolutely irrelevant to one's position in society. Most Jews have a particular affinity for universal values. This arises from their own marginal relationship to the general society, as well as from the Jewish community itself. Consequently, they insist that only achieved or ethnically neutral characteristics (such as intellect or reason) are relevant to one's role or status. If Negroness or

Jewishness has something to do with being a teacher, the Jew fears he may become an object of discrimination; equally important, he is not able to escape the condition of his Jewishness. Of course, he does not want to cease being a Jew. But he wants to restrict his Jewishness to the synagogue or philanthropic activity. The rest of the time he wants to be the same as everybody else. But this also means that everybody else cannot be labeled "Negro" or "Christian," for otherwise the Jew becomes a "Jew." So everybody else has got to be Doctor, Lawyer, Garbage Collector, or Musician; then the Jew can "disappear."

How do Jews respond to the new black militancy? Again, the structure of the response is as important as its content. Jews have two alternatives: either to oppose Negro demands[5] or to work out some accommodation. But that accommodation can only be based on recognition of the right of Negroes to press particularistic or racial demands upon those aspects of the American system which have until now been considered outside the bounds of pluralist accommodation: professional or occupational values. A survivalist might, in fact, welcome Negro demands precisely because they serve to break down the monolithic pressure of Americanism, which necessarily erodes Jewish identity. Before the Jewish community as such could make accommodations, it would have to unify its communal authority. This would anticipate the emergence of Jewish leaders who are far more self-conscious about the Jewish component within American society. Indeed, the most committed, survivalistic Jews have just the qualities necessary to negotiate with Negro militants. Unlike the integrationists, they have a high degree of sensitivity to anti-Semitism and readily recognize the phenomenon when they encounter it. But they are neither as shocked, outraged, or frustrated as are the modal American Jews (those who stand near the center of the integrationist-survivalist continuum) by its presence. They have a higher degree of tolerance for anti-Semitism precisely because they accept it as a fact of life.

An integrationist response to black militancy would simply deny the relevance of the Negro threat to Jews. The president of a Students for a Democratic Society (SDS) chapter, asked to comment on Dick Gregory's remarks about "Jewish slumlords and price gougers," said he did not feel that Gregory was anti-Semitic in intent or substance.[6] Another Jewish SDS member from Berkeley was quoted as saying:

I don't like it when they say "We're going to take over this country and paint it black." They spend half their time attacking the white liberals as sellouts. But I think it is incumbent on us to be accommodating because of their subjugation. It's just a stage they're passing through.[7]

There were Jews who agreed with SNCC (Student Nonviolent Coordinating Committee) when in 1967 it attacked Israel as an outpost of American imperialism, defending the Arabs and attacking the Jews. This is a good example of an integrationist approach. The Jewish leftist feels so secure in his American identity that he does not perceive anti-Semitism as a threat to his own welfare.[8] As the author of a study of the New Left concludes, "to white radicals, including Jews, the question of whether Jews are the special object of black hostility seems irrelevant. They are telling us that all of society in its present form is evil and must be destroyed."[9]

Neither the survivalist nor the integrationist response is characteristic of the organized Jewish community. It has responded in an ad hoc fashion, because its dilemma of integration-survival precludes ideological clarity. From a survivalist perspective, Jewish organizations are quite sensitive to manifestations of Negro anti-Semitism. In 1968, New York University appointed a Negro, John Hatchett, as director of its Afro-American student center. Six months earlier Hatchett had published an article attacking "anti-black Jewish educators" who abused the family and culture of black children in addition to miseducating them. When the article first appeared, the American Jewish Congress, the Catholic Interracial Council, and the Protestant Council of the City of New York condemned it as "black nazism." Most major Jewish organizations protested NYU's appointment of Hatchett. Significantly, the New York Civil Liberties Union, which has a particular attraction for integrationist Jews, defended the appointment on the grounds that "a man's right to employment must be based on his professional performance, not on his private thoughts, words, beliefs or associations; university employees should be appointed solely on the basis of ability and competence in their professional fields."[10]

Jewish organizations, however, eschew such professional or universalistic values when confronted by an openly identifiable anti-Semite. At the other end of the spectrum, the organized Jewish community has continued to battle for equal protection for Negroes. It is sympathetic to Negro charges of governmental and private discrimination, and it urges large-scale public and private investments for Negro housing, jobs, and education. Such demands are pressed in terms of liberal and humanitarian, rather than ethnic, values.

But these responses to specific issues do not resolve the Jewish problem of a generalized orientation to the primary Negro demands for power, local control, and the allocation of employment, political appointments, and money on the basis of the Negro community's having a quasi-corporate status. The Jewish parallel is readily seen; for example, the American Jewish Committee has pointed to the absence of Jews in the top echelons of corporations, banks, insurance companies, and universities as sufficient evidence of discrimination. While this may seem consistent with Negro demands for a more proportionate number of jobs as school principals and civil-service workers, the demands of each group are really mutually exclusive. The Negro community demands Negro principals in Negro schools on the grounds that only the Negro can understand the real needs of the Negro child. Similarly, the gentile board of a large corporation argues that it cannot appoint Jews to top positions because the executive role involves personal interrelationships in a social setting in which the Jew could not function effectively. Both the Negroes and the corporate leaders thus justify their demands in particularistic terms. Jews are to be displaced by Negroes and denied employment, but for ascriptive rather than achievement reasons; this goes completely against the whole thrust of Jewish accommodation to American society. The Jews are far too integrationist to recognize the legitimacy of Negro claims for relevance of ascriptive characteristics. This would probably be true even if it were not the Jews themselves who were to be displaced. Jews are also too survivalistic to ignore the existence of Negro anti-Semitism. How, then, other than through blanket opposition, can most Jews accommodate themselves to black militancy?

Jews have a second problem in orienting themselves to the new Negro community without betraying their own liberal political values, their sympathy for the underdog, and their tradition of helping the Negro. They see themselves as having become integrated into American society and the modern world on an individual basis. They perceive this integration as being accompanied by a relaxation of group norms and a narrowing of the scope of Jewish identity to a religious setting. This is now threatened by Negro demands for communal recognition in heretofore ethnically neutral areas. The Negro community, for example, demands the right to make its own appointments and to control jobs allocated to Negroes, rather than having "experts" from the general society select the Negro. Not only are Negro schools to have Negro principals, but the principals are to be selected by the Negro community. In 1968 black militants not only demanded a Negro mayor in Newark, but they also insisted that he be selected by them rather than by the traditional parties. Consciously or unconsciously, the specter of this happening to the Jews as well is most frightening to the integrationist-survivalist Jews. So it is not surprising that the Jewish community has so much difficulty in orienting itself to the new Negro presence.

THE PAROCHIALISM-HUMANISM PROBLEM

It is assumed that within most if not all people there lies a religious impulse. This is the impulse to reach out to God, to the "totally other," to some force or power which is seen as controlling one's destiny and as giving meaning and purpose to one's life. While there are certain universal elements which are common to the expression of this impulse, there are also particularistic elements which are culturally and temporally conditioned. Institutionalized religion, through its sanctums, rituals, and sacred texts, has generally defined itself in form and content as the most exalted expression of the religious impulse and as the response of God to that impulse. Institutional religion requires its members to continue to find expression for their religious needs through it. The religious impulse, however, often breaks through the constraints of institutional religion. At the minimum, the institution claims exclusive authority to judge the legitimacy of a religious expression, that is, the right to determine whether a particular expression indeed reflects a valid religious impulse. In prosaic terms, it could be said that the institutional efficacy of a religious group might best be measured by its ability to impose its judgment authoritatively on the legitimacy or validity of a religious expression. If the institution cannot do that, it does not matter how many members or churches or ministers it has. A religious institution may seek to incorporate a new religious expression into its own structure rather than deny its legitimacy, but it *must* respond.

The religious impulse of some young Americans in the 1960s found expression in social action: the war on poverty, civil rights, the Peace Corps, Vista, and opposition to the war in Vietnam. It is probable that not even a majority of those involved in social action did so for religious reasons which they were aware of or which they associated with a particular religious institution. Many others who observed from the sidelines wondered whether the social-action movements were a legitimate expression of a religious impulse. Religious institutions were called upon to appraise the social-action movements in terms of their own religious traditions and their own conceptions of right and wrong.

This created special problems for the Jews. True, the goal of social justice is present in the basic structure of Jewish religious thought, so social-action movements (particularly those that operated within the law) presented no dogmatic problems. In addition, the liberal political orientation of American Jews is congenial to the political goals of the social-action movements. Moreover, the movement certainly met the integrationist needs of American Jews, by identifying them with participation in American life through an activity upon which Protestant and Catholic circles also conferred legitimacy. But these needs make social action a highly problematic form of religious expression. The difficulty is that because social action can become a way of life, by commanding the total involvement of an individual, it cuts across institutional boundaries and makes particularistic religious preoccupations appear trivial. Christianity is not threatened by the breakdown of institutional differences. A religious impulse which seeks expression sooner or later will locate itself in the dominant religious tradition of the nation. But once a Jew finds religious expression outside his institutional framework, he is less likely to return to his traditional camp.

Second, the religious impulse in Judaism is expressed primarily through the study of legal codes and texts and adherence to them. Finding this too constraining at times, Jewish religiosity broke through in the past to express itself in other forms, such as particularly devout worship, singing and dancing, mysticism, and belief in false Messiahs. Some of these expressions were in turn incorporated into normative Judaism; others were rejected. The crucial factor was whether each of these expressions was compatible with Jewish law. Social action is superficially compatible with Jewish law, but its life-style is not. One can—but one does not—drop out of a freedom march because it is taking place on the Sabbath or Yom Kippur. One does not measure the risk of arrest and incarceration in a southern prison in terms of the availability of kosher food. One does not refuse to participate in a voter registration meeting because it is interjected into a Christian worship service. One does not refuse to work with African tribes or South American Indians because one cannot find a quorum of Jews there with whom one can pray. Most importantly, a young couple, after working together and developing a mutual dependence, do not resist love and marriage because one is a Jew and the other is a Gentile.

The structure of social action, therefore, requires a choice between its own life-style and the norms of traditional Judaism. For the purely survivalist or the purely integrationist Jew, there is no dilemma. To a Jewish community torn between survival and integration the problem at present has no resolution. One alternative would be *Jewish* social action, that is, Jewish participation in an organized effort, so that the Jew need not sacrifice the more institutionalized expression of the religious impulse to the more universalist ones. It is disappointing to some that the Jewish community has generally not sought to organize such activity. Where it has, however, it has not found enthusiastic participants. Survivalist youths have their special concerns for Israel or Soviet Jewry. To integrationists it would be ludicrous to create particularist organizations to accomplish the identical goals that universalist groups seek. To the integrationist-survivalist, particularistic groups in the realm of social action are self-defeating, because politics is a crucial area for expressing integrationist rather than survivalist values. A few individuals have found their Jewish identity through social action. But this has not been the experience of most Jews.

3

THE RELIGION OF AMERICAN JEWS

While it has been noted that the integration-survival tension is crucial in the formation of Jewish identity, the content of that identity has not been specified. This is a difficult and highly speculative task. Clearly, at least for most Jews, it is neither cultural nor national. If it were cultural, we could not explain the Jewish community's general neglect of Jewish education and culture or the elevation to prominence within the community of people who are Jewishly illiterate. If it were national, we would not only see more Jews willing to emigrate to Israel, but we would also find more sympathy for those who negate Jewish life in the Diaspora. We would also see some demand for Jewish autonomy in American political and economic life. This is totally absent. Jews are even uncomfortable with the notion of a formal channel of communication between American political leaders and representative Jewish leaders. This stems from a denial of the existence of a Jewish political community and of Jewish political leaders, itself an indication of the absence of national concerns.Perhaps, as we shall suggest later in this chapter, Jewish identity is, at bottom, familistic and social. Yet in its public posture, and in some respects in its private posture as well, Jewish self-identity is religious. However, it is religious in a sense that is peculiar to American Jews.

Contemporary American Judaism is the creation of the East European Jew whose Jewish identity as a member of a communal, rather than a religious, group was formed before he came to the United States. But in America, communal identity lacked legitimacy. It took the Jew some time to appreciate this, but it became more apparent as he became increasingly acculturated to American values and standards. In this process two things occurred. First, Jewish communal identity became more attenuated. Second, with the decline of ethnic ties among other immigrant groups, such as the Irish, Italians, and Poles, the Jews, who retained a much stronger sense of communality, were increasingly conscious of their variance from American standards. This is the problem of American Jewry. The major institutions of American Judaism must be understood, not only as efforts to resolve the integration-survival tension, but also as the outgrowth of efforts to resolve the tension between what the East European Jew knew he was and what America assumed him to be.

The price of integration into American life is the pursuit of communal behavior patterns to which the society grants legitimacy. It is, for example, all right for a religious group to establish an educational system of day schools or supplementary schools, but it is not all right for a political party or a national minority to do so. Most Americans are not antagonized by the existence of Catholic parochial schools, nor would they object if enrollment in such schools was limited to Catholics. They would find it quite understandable if such schools taught Latin, since this might be necessary for liturgical purposes. But what would they think if Italians established their own school systems, limited enrollment to the children of Italian-born parents or grandparents, and stressed the study of the Italian language and history? They would consider such schools divisive and un-American because they do not consider nationality a legitimate basis for exclusiveness. Religious exclusiveness, however, is accepta-

ble. And to the extent that religion also bears a culture, it legiti-
mizes a cultural exclusiveness.

Most Americans who are conscious of the fact probably respect, or at least accept, the fact that Judaism prohibits intermarriage between Jew and non-Jew. Rabbis are not considered
bigoted for refusing to officiate at an intermarriage ceremony.
After all, "That's their religion." Furthermore, even if the religion itself is suspected of bigotry, one may develop an understandable position based on the argument that the individual is
not accountable for the tenets of his faith. For example, Americans may believe that Catholicism is intolerant for insisting that
the non-Catholic spouse in a Catholic marriage promise to raise
any future offspring as Catholics. But the individual Catholic is
not blamed for this doctrine. On the contrary, he might even
elicit respect for remaining religiously loyal despite the obviously unsatisfactory (that is, un-American) aspects of his religion. The fault lies in the religion, not in the man.

But what would be said about an Irish father who opposed his
daughter's marriage to an Italian, a Democrat to a Republican,
a northerner to a southerner, or a Negro to a white? That is
bigotry. It is not legitimate. It is an act for which the individual
is held responsible. It would be quite insufficient to protest that
if one wants to preserve Irishness or Democratness or northern-
ness or whiteness, one cannot sanction intermarriage. Like
gefilte fish, pizza, chow mein, and mint juleps, they may have
been the creation of one particular group, but now they must
be equally accessible to all Americans.

These few examples suggest what happened to the East
European Jew and his descendants in America. The East
European came with his Judaism already defined in communal terms. He came with a desire to preserve his identity,
but he also wanted acceptance and legitimacy for his institutions. He could not legitimize institutions of exclusiveness
which were defined in communal-ethnic-cultural-national
terms. But an alternative was available. Judaism already existed in the United States before the East European came.

Its predominant expression was Reform, which meant that its self-definition was already religious. If Americans reflected on Judaism at all, they must have assumed it was like Christianity, that is, a religion. Furthermore, within the self-definition of the East European Jew, the religious element was also present. One can hardly blame the Jew, therefore, for taking the easiest way out of his dilemma—calling Judaism a religion for external and formal purposes and filling the form with ethnic or communal content.

This is not to suggest that the immigrant was aware of this process. Precisely because he was not aware of it, he came to believe in the reality of his own public image. American Jews do believe they are practicing a religion which is conceptually similar to Christianity. To the extent that they continue to believe this, they continue reshaping Judaism to fit this belief. Indeed, this is precisely what the third and fourth generation of American Jews have done. But as yet, and despite the changes which will be cited later, Judaism still remains something quite different conceptually from Christianity.

FOLK AND ELITE RELIGION

We have already suggested that the integration-survival tension led American Jews to define themselves as a religion. We will further suggest that the integration-survival values led to particular forms of religious behavior and beliefs among American Jews. However, in order to understand fully the religion of American Jews we must embark on a brief theoretical detour and define two new concepts: "folk religion" and "elite religion."

In chapter 1 we defined *folk* religion as the religion of a community which delineates the peculiarity of the particular group and which is generated by the community itself. This was contrasted with *universal* religion, in which the individual rather than the collectivity is the object of the religion. In this chapter folk religion will be defined somewhat differently and juxtaposed, not with universal religion, but rather with what shall be termed *elite* religion.[1]

The popular religious culture of folk religion can be better understood if we first understand elite religion. The term religion refers here to a formal organized institution with acknowledged leaders. Within the institution, symbols and rituals are acknowledged as legitimate expressions or reenactments of religious experience, and a set of beliefs is articulated as ultimate truths.[2] Elite religion is the symbols and rituals (the cult) and beliefs which the leaders acknowledge as legitimate. But most importantly, elite religion is also the religious organization itself, its hierarchical arrangements, the authority of the leaders and their source of authority, and the rights and obligations of the followers to the organization and its leaders.

For various reasons—the evolution of religion, the conflict of different cultures, differentiated levels of religious and even nonreligious education, and psychological propensities—large numbers of people may affiliate with a particular religious institution, and even identify themselves as part of that religion, without really accepting all aspects of its elitist formulation. What is more, a kind of subculture may exist within a religion which the acknowledged leaders ignore or even condemn, but in which a majority of the members participate. This is called folk religion. Why consider folk and elite religion to be two aspects of the same religion? Why not call them two separate religions? The answer is that both share the same organization and at least nominally recognize the authoritative nature of the cult and beliefs articulated by the elite religion. Folk religion is not self-conscious; it does not articulate its own rituals and beliefs or demand recognition for its informal leaders. As far as elite religion is concerned, folk religion is not a movement but an error, or a set of errors, shared by many people.

Folk religion is expressed primarily though rituals and symbols. These rituals may be rooted in superstition; they may originate from an older localized religion which has been replaced by the elite religion; or they may arise from a need on the part of people for the sanctification of certain social, economic, or even sexual activity which elite religion refuses to legitimize. Folk religion tends to accept the organizational structure of the elite religion but to be indifferent to the elite belief structure. Of course, its rituals and symbols imply a belief system, but this tends to be mythic rather than rational and hence not in opposition to the more complex theological elaboration of the elite religion. Where the beliefs of the folk religion are self-conscious and articulated, they tend to be beliefs about which the elite religion is neutral. For example, the fact that the folk religion of American Jews affirms a belief in the separation of church and state as a cardinal principle of Judaism creates no problems as long as the elite religion doesn't claim the opposite.

I do not want to elaborate on the interrelationships between folk religion and elite religion. It is clear that they are characterized by continual tensions. The potential for folk religion to become institutionalized always exists; if it does, it will become a separate religion or an official heresy. The history of Catholicism is filled with such examples. Yet folk religion permits a more intimate religious expression and experience for many people, and may, in fact, integrate them into organizational channels of the elite religion. It is a mistake to think of folk religion as necessarily more primitive than elite religion. While its ceremonies and sanctums evoke emotions and inchoate ideas associated with basic instincts and primitive emotions, it is also more flexible than elite religion. Hence it is also capable of developing ceremonial responses to contemporary needs which may be incorporated into the elite religion. Much religious liturgy arises from the folk religion and is incorporated into the elite religion.

The absence of an elaborate theology within folk religion and the appeal of folk religion to primal instincts and emotions does not mean that folk religion is less attractive to intellectuals than is elite religion. Quite the opposite may be true under certain circumstances. In secular America, elite religion has been forced to retreat before the challenge of science, biblical scholarship, notions of relativism implicit in contemporary social science, and the whole mood of current intellectual life.

The foundations of religion are most critically shaken in the area of the doctrines and beliefs which elite religious leaders have formulated in order to rationalize religious organization cult. The problem for the religious elite has been that most intellectuals cannot accept dogmatic formulations which purport to be true or to have arisen independent of time and place. Hence intellectuals have special difficulty with elite religion. But the same intellectual currents which challenge religious doctrine can also serve to defend behavioral and even organizational forms against the onslaught of such secular doctrines as twentieth-century positivism or eighteenth- and nineteenth-century deism. Thus folk religion, with its stress on customary behavior and traditional practices, may be legitimized functionally without an elitist prop. An intellectual today may well be attracted to folk religion because it provides him with comfort and solace, a sense of tradition, a feeling of rootedness, a source of family unity. His world view may remain secular, and from the point of view of elite religion his beliefs will therefore be quite unsatisfactory. But it is, at least in the first instance, elite religion, not folk, which is challenged by his world view.

In traditional Judaism, folk religion has always existed side by side with elite religion. Many of its ceremonies and rituals were incorporated into the elite religion; others were rejected; still others achieved a kind of quasi-incorporation. They were and are widely practiced and even have a certain liturgical legitimacy; but they are still outside the boundaries of elite religion. Such ceremonies, for example, are associated with Jewish holidays. Best known, perhaps, are Jewish New Year rituals of eating apple and honey and the ceremony of tashlich, at which Jews throw crumbs representing their sins into a body of water. The essentially healthy relationship between the folk and elite religion in traditional Judaism is exemplified by the fact that Jews who participate in tashlich feel the need to accompany the act with the recitation of a traditional psalm. That is, the sanctums of the elite religion must accompany a purely folk religious act.

Every religious group has both its folk and elitist aspect. They may differ from one another, and, as we shall see, branches or denominations within Judaism do differ from one another as to the extent to which the folk and elite formulations are in tension with each other. But first some historical background is necessary.

AMERICAN JUDAISM BEFORE THE TURN OF THE CENTURY

In 1880 there were approximately 250,000 Jews in the United States. During the next forty years over 2,000,000 Jews immigrated, the great majority from Eastern Europe. The intensity of the immigrants' Jewish identification and Jewish concerns, and even more, their large numbers and the problems created by such a vast lower-class segment of people, overwhelmed the existing Jewish institutions and transformed the very nature of American Judaism. Consequently, the turn of the century is a convenient starting place for anyone who wishes to understand the roots of the contemporary Jewish community.

Early Reform

Before the arrival of the East Europeans, most American Jews were German in origin and Reform in religious orientation. But there was a great difference between American Reform and the German Reform to which we referred in the first chapter. German Reform represented a conscious break with the Jewish tradition. Under the influence of the European Enlightenment and concerned with the requirements for Jewish emancipation, it defined itself in opposition to the traditional patterns of Jewish belief and practice. It was a new elitist formulation of Judaism. In contrast, American Reform was the religious organization of the German-American Jew who came searching for personal liberty and economic advancement. That Jew was neither ideologically oriented nor purposefully assimilationist. He had no need to rebel consciously against the tradition, because there were no traditional institutions in the United States which were of any concern to him. American Reform at its outset was the folk religion of the German-American Jew.

Jews had lived here prior to the large German immigration, which began in the 1840s. They included Sephardic Jews (Jews of Spanish descent) and Germanic Jews, who came in numbers small enough to be assimilated into Sephardic institutions. But these institutions, centered around the synagogue, were confined mostly to the east coast, were wealthy, followed traditional Sephardic practices quite different from those of the Germans, and were indifferent, if not hostile, to the new German immigrants.

The new immigrants, many of whom settled away from the older Sephardic communities, naturally established their own synagogues. At least, those who bothered about Judaism did so. But they did not think of these institutions as particularly denominational. The new German synagogues were not established in deliberate opposition to any other synagogue or ideology. With the arrival of German rabbis, preeminently Isaac Mayer Wise, who was already identified with German Reform, some deliberate and successful efforts were made toward organizing these synagogues into a central body with a uniform liturgy and a single ideology.

In 1857 Wise published a prayer book which he hoped would meet the needs of these congregations. He called it *Minhag America*, the custom of America. To Wise, Jewish denominationalism was not the division between Reform and Orthodoxy. At this period in his life Wise believed that the only type of synagogue which would survive was the indigenous American congregation, which he saw as naturally Reform in orientation. Wise did not fear the opposition of Orthodox or traditionalist Jews. The great Jewish problem in America was not to fight the tradition but to retain the Jewish allegiance of the immigrants and their children. Consequently, Wise thought of his prayer book and liturgy as reflecting, not so much Reform, but rather the needs of American Jews.

In 1873 Wise founded the Union of American Hebrew Congregations and in 1875, Hebrew Union College (HUC) for the training of American rabbis. The word Union in the name is significant because it suggests the absence of schism. As Samuel Cohon has noted, the term Union expressed the founder's hope "to have one theological school for all Jews of the country,"[3] at least for all but the "ultra-Orthodox," to use Cohon's formulation. Certain segments of American Judaism found the practices of HUC "too Reform," however, and in 1886 they founded the Jewish Theological Seminary Association to organize a more traditional institution to train rabbis. Even then an Orthodox leader, Judah David Eisenstein, objected to the new Seminary, and argued that if HUC was indeed too Reform, one solution was for the non-Reform to identify themselves with it and change its character.[4]

American Reform, however, had already begun to take shape as a distinctive movement with its own ideological position. In 1885 a group of Reform rabbis met in Pittsburgh and adopted the famous statement of principle known as the Pittsburgh Platform. These rabbis represented the more radical and ideological wing of Reform. Wise himself was not present at the meeting. But after 1885 and until the repudiation of the Pittsburgh Platform in 1937 by the Central Conference of American Rabbis (the Reform rabbinical organization), this statement represented, one might say, the elitist formulation of American Reform.[5] It repudiated the binding character of "Mosaic legislation," that is, Jewish law and its divine revelation. It is doubtful, however, if this rejection of traditional Jewish law and dogma was more shocking to the sensibilities of the East European immigrant than the assertions that Judaism was *only* a religion; that "we consider ourselves no longer a nation but a religious community"; and that "we recognize in Judaism a progressive religion, ever striving to be in accord with the postulates of reason." This was the spirit of American Reform which the East European Jew found upon his arrival in the United States.

The New Immigrants

Who were the new immigrants? The important fact to be noted is that a disproportionately large number of them, relative to a cross-section of East European Jewry, were nontraditionalists, secularist Jews, Socialists, and Zionists. A few of them, particularly the Socialists, were militantly antireligious. Most, however, were not ideologically oriented. They were traditionalist in orientation but without the political, economic, or ideological stake that many East European Jewish leaders had in traditionalism. They were adherents of the folk, rather than the elite, religion of traditionalism.

Within traditional Judaism, folk religion and elite religion may be distinguished from each other by their orientation to change. Traditional society differs from modern society, not in the occurrence of change (all societies change), but in its orientation to the concept of change.[6] Traditionalists accept only change which can be legitimized by past values and practices. The hallmark of the elite religion of traditional Judaism is the fact that the touchstone of legitimacy is the sacred textual tradition and the codes of Jewish law. The traditional elite are represented by the talmudic scholars and sages. The traditionalist folk, on the other hand, find the touchstone of legitimacy in the practices of the community. In this sense the traditionalist folk are more innately conservative than the elite but are more susceptible to a radical break with the past, once the consensus within the community is broken

The first traditionalist immigrants found themselves surrounded by a disproportionate number of nontraditionalists. Not only were the vast majority of new immigrants adherents of folk, rather than elite, traditionalism, but there was also a decided absence of distinguished scholars and rabbis. Israel Rosenberg, one of the leading Orthodox East European rabbis in America, noted the miserable state of Jewish education and commented at the 1924 convention of the Union of Orthodox Rabbis (Agudat Horabbonim): "To a certain extent the Jews of Europe are also responsible for this situation. When they saw that the stream of emigration to America was increasing, it was incumbent among them to send us the spiritual giants, those who had it in their powers to influence and to work."[7]

Although most of the estimated fifty thousand Jews who immigrated to the United States from 1881 to 1885 settled in New York, the leading East European congregation of the city had only a part-time rabbi of meager scholarship. When twenty-six Orthodox congregations met to choose a joint leader for New York Jewry, no American rabbi was even considered. In 1887 the secretary to Rabbi Isaac Elhanan Spektor, the outstanding rabbinic authority from Russia, referred to American rabbinical leaders as "improper men."[8] The few talmudic scholars who did come "were without honor or support even in their own poor communities."[9] One contemporary, commenting on the talmudic saying that "the sages are kings," noted that in America this should read "the shoemakers, tailors, and usurers are the sages."[10]

The absence of a religious elite meant that the traditionalist immigrants were especially susceptible to a breakdown in religious consensus. To a greater extent than ever, the folk now set their own standards independently of the elite. The traditionalist immigrants were certainly not irreligious, nor did they wish to conceal their Jewish identity. But they did desire to be accepted and integrated into American society. As East Europeans they viewed their Judaism in communal-ethnic terms. Their world was divided into Irish, Italians, Poles, Jews, and so on, not Catholics, Protestants, and Jews. And while they were not irreligious, neither were they religious in the elitist sense in which one's life is bounded and guided by a legal textual tradition. Their piety was what Leo Baeck called *Milieu-Fromigkeit*, and what we have called a manifestation of folk religion. Willing as they were to take extended leave of family and home, they were less committed to tradition and more accepting of new values than their relatives and neighbors who came much later.

When the rabbi of Slutsk visited America and appeared at a public meeting of the Union of Orthodox Jewish Congregations during the first wave of immigration, "he chastised the assemblage for having emigrated to this *trefa* [impure] land."[11] Similarly, would-be emigrants were warned by such renowned rabbinic authorities as the Hafetz Hayim, Rabbi Israel Meir Hacohen, to stay home and not endanger their Judaism.[12] Those who did emigrate were unable to separate the distinctively religious or legally essential elements from the nonessential elements of Judaism. We find that the "religious" practices which persisted among the immigrants were those most closely associated with the cultural life-style of Eastern Europe and were irrelevant to the process of American acculturation. In contrast, practices which were more deeply rooted in the textual religious tradition were readily abandoned.

Among the most important set of rituals in Jewish law are those surrounding Sabbath observance. The Torah commands the Jew, under penalty of death, to refrain from work on the Sabbath. The Sabbath rest is connected to creation itself. By resting on the Sabbath, the Jew refreshes and renews his spirit through prayer, study, good food, and even sexual intercourse, to which he is commanded. In the elitist formulation the Jew also affirms, by abstinence from forbidden work, his belief in God the Creator, who also rested on the Sabbath. But Sabbath observance entailed economic hardship for the immigrants and often did not survive the voyage across the Atlantic. A survey of Jewish workmen on the Lower East Side revealed that only 25 percent rested on the Sabbath; 60 percent of the stores owned by Jews were open.[13] Similar conditions prevailed among the immigrants in England, where a Jewish minister commented that "a friend of mine, who refused to work on the Sabbath and suffered on account of his staunchness, told me that he was reproached with being like a 'greener.' "[14]

Kashrut, the laws pertaining to permissible and forbidden foods, survived longer than Sabbath observance, though in an attenuated form. The parts which survived were rooted in the folk, rather than in the elitist, aspects of Judaism. The laws of kashrut govern which animals may be consumed, as well as which cuts of meat may be eaten, and prohibit mixing dairy and meat dishes. Kashrut resulted, therefore, in certain styles of food. Long after most Jews ceased to observe kashrut they continued to eat "kosher style." Among the animals which are forbidden to the Jew is the pig. In the elitist formulation eating pork products is sinful, but no more sinful than eating shrimp. Further, the laws make no distinction between consuming forbidden foods in one's home and consuming them in a restaurant. But the folk religion made both these distinctions. Pig was anathema, and it is not uncommon today to find Jews who will eat all nonkosher food except pork. Similarly, a newly emerging folk religion of American Judaism gave special sanctity to the home and forbade eating certain foods in the intimacy of the family but not outside. Many new immigrants in particular would have been shocked at the thought of eating nonkosher meat at home *or* outside long after they ceased observing the Sabbath. Behind all this is the special association between eating and cultural or life-style patterns which the Jew retained.

An elitist Jew might be expected to provide extensive Jewish education for his child, but as late as 1916 there were only two religious elementary schools (yeshivot) in the United States.

According to an educator of that period, Jews opposed parochial schools, which they felt were harmful to democracy.[15] Less than 24 percent of the estimated number of Jewish children of elementary school age in New York received any form of Jewish education in 1917, and less than 1 percent received any training at the high school level.[16] It was primarily the elderly or the very poor who studied the Talmud, and then only at a very low level.

Jewish law extends to the most intimate details of family life —laws of family purity—and requires a married woman to immerse herself in a lustral bath (mikvah) at a specified time following each menstrual period. Writing in 1928 about the immigrant era, an observer commented that lustral baths were simply unavailable and that "the daughters of Israel had ceased to guard their purity."[17] The Union of Orthodox Rabbis, in the first issue of their publication in 1918, noted that family purity had been "erased from our lives." Requirements of family purity did not involve economic hardship, but they were an anachronism in the values of middle-class American culture toward which the immigrants aspired.

Many Jews did retain an attachment to the synagogue, but this was a broadly cultural, rather than a specifically religious, commitment. As early as 1887 one commentator noted that when the immigrants had built beautiful synagogues they felt they had fulfilled their obligation to Judaism.[18] The large majority of Jews attended a synagogue only on Yom Kippur, the most sacred day in the Jewish calendar.

The new immigrants did found countless small synagogues almost immediately upon arrival, but that in itself was no evidence of religiosity. If the function of the synagogue was primarily for worship there was no need for such proliferation. But if its primary purpose was to meet the social and cultural needs of small groups originating in different European communities this proliferation is more understandable. The synagogues were social forums and benevolent societies adapted to the requirements of poor, unacculturated people. The evidence suggests an absence of religious, as distinct from ethnic, commitment on the part of the East European immigrants to the United States. But the older Jewish community made no such distinctions. To them the bulk of the immigrants were very religious unacculturated Jews.

The New Immigrants and the Older American Jewish Establishment

There was more than a difference of Jewish identity or self-conception separating the new immigrants from the existing religious establishment in the United States. There were differences in social class and class culture which prevented cooperation between the traditionalist East European immigrants and even the non-Reform Americanized religious personalities who founded such institutions as the Jewish Theological Seminary. The former group, no less than the latter, desired integration and denied any contradiction between integration and survival. But the two groups differed markedly in the actual state of their integration and acculturation. Only the carriers of the elite religion, the rabbinical leaders of the East European Jews, saw the strain between integration and survival. Their error lay in their inability to distinguish religious survival from the survival of the patterns and folkways of Eastern Europe.

The major subgroup among the Americanized non-Reform Jews consisted of the members of Sephardic synagogues (preeminent among them Shearith Israel of New York and Mikveh Israel of Philadelphia), who associated their religious tradition with a class aristocracy. Most of these people, even before 1900, were of Ashkenazic European rather than Sephardic descent, but they assimilated and sought to emulate the cultural patterns of the high-status Sephardim. Their identification with traditional Judaism was analogous to the association of the English aristocracy with Anglicanism, although even in those syna-

gogues the desire for change away from tradition was noticeable before the turn of the century. Thus, even among the
upper-class Jews there was an attachment to folk, as distinct
from elite, religion. But regardless of their self-definition or
degree of religiosity, all upper-class Jews were highly acculturated and integrated into American life.

A second ethnic-cultural subgroup among the non-Reform
American Jewish groups was a small group of Germans. Most of
these Germans probably came from Poland or Austria-Hungary, but they are identified as Germans because prior to their
immigration they had been trained in German-style schools,
they spoke German, and they generally felt most at home in
Germanic culture. Most of the Jews from Germany in the
United States were Reform, and one suspects (although the data
are not available), that the traditionalist Germans were from
Poland or Austria-Hungary. In any event, they did have a few
traditional congregations of their own.

The representative institution of the old American non-
Reform Jews at the time of mass immigration was the Jewish
Theological Seminary of America. Its first president, Sabato
Morais, a Sephardic leader, proposed naming the institution
"The Orthodox Seminary." After Morais's death, the active
heads of the Seminary were Bernard Drachman and Henry
Pereira Mendes; the latter was at that time the leading Sephardic rabbi in the country. Besides his role in the Seminary,
Mendes was president of the New York Board of Jewish Ministers, a forerunner of the New York Board of Rabbis, which
included Reform rabbis but no Orthodox traditional rabbis from
the Lower East Side.[19] Mendes's attitude to the East European
synagogues is reflected in this public statement: "We have to
choose between striving for learning and culture, or allow these
communities to honor learning of but one kind in their own
peculiar way, to maintain services which show little love of
culture and which repel, methods which fail in the second generation."[20] His private sentiments about the cultural patterns of

the East European traditionalist were reputed to be even more derisive.

Most upper-class traditionalists were unwilling to associate with the lower-class traditionalists. Perhaps they thought that the cultural obstinacy of the latter group doomed their future. Perhaps they feared that their own social status would be threatened by such a gesture. More critically, the two traditionalist segments shared less in common than might otherwise have been the case, because each emphasized its own folk conception of traditional Judaism rather than a common elitist formulation. In Europe, in contrast, Agudat Israel was able to unite traditionalists of both East and West because it represented an elitist formulation of traditional Judaism. In America, however, cultural and class differences proved more significant than commitments to tradition.

THE RISE OF CONSERVATIVE JUDAISM

We are now in a position to understand the emergence of a distinctly American brand of Judaism. American Judaism in its religious aspects is not quite synonymous with Conservative Judaism, but it is intimately connected with its growth.

In 1902 the Jewish Theological Seminary was reorganized, and Solomon Schechter was brought from England to head it. Its new financial benefactors were primarily nontraditionalists (Reform Jews) who hoped that the institution and its future rabbinical graduates would Americanize and acculturate the East European immigrants. It is most interesting that the Reform Jews sought to use a nominally traditionalist institution to reach the new immigrant. However, their own status in American society was threatened by the masses of Jewish immigrants.[21] Indeed, the rising anti-Semitism in this period was attributed to the nonacculturated character of the immigrants which reflected unfavorably on the native American Jews.[22] They apparently believed that the Seminary could reach the new immigrants since it shared their commitment to religious tradition.

In 1913 the Seminary leadership and its Alumni Association created a suprasynagogue organization, the United Synagogue of America, which was to become the congregational arm of Conservative Judaism. Its laity would in time depart from the religious standards of traditional Judaism, folk and elite. But at the time of its founding, even the Conservative nature of the new group was not clear. A projected name for the new organization, "a Union of Conservative Congregations, was objected to as being too sectarian."[23]

The United Synagogue of America was founded by delegates from 22 congregations. By 1970 it had approximately 850 synagogue affiliates. Another 100 congregations were identified with Conservative Judaism, although for one reason or another they were not members of the United Synagogue. A very rough estimate of the number of Jews affiliated with these congregations would be one and a half million, compared to about one million Jews affiliated with Reform congregations and about three-quarters of a million affiliated or identified with Orthodox congregations.

Not all Jews affiliated with Conservative synagogues consider themselves to be Conservative Jews. But many Jews who are members of Reform or Orthodox congregations or who are not affiliated with any synagogue label themselves Conservative. A study of members of Orthodox synagogues in Washington Heights, the upper portion of Manhattan, showed that 40 percent of those on mailing lists of Orthodox congregations considered themselves to be Conservative Jews.[24] It is difficult to estimate with any accuracy the proportion of American Jews who identify themselves as Conservative, since we lack any reliable data for New York and its suburbs, where over 40 percent of the American Jews are located. There are, however, a number of recent community studies for other Jewish population centers. Surveys of Washington, D.C., Providence, Los Angeles, Detroit, Milwaukee, and Boston show a fair degree of consistency in the percentage of Jews who report themselves as Orthodox, Conservative, or Reform.[25] For the Orthodox, the figure hovers around 16 percent, although in Milwaukee it is as high as 22 percent. For Reform, the figure is around 25 percent, reaching as high as 29 percent in Los Angeles. The spread is much greater for Conservatives, ranging from 35 percent in Los Angeles (where 24 percent of the respondents refused to identify themselves by denomination) to a high of 55 percent in Providence.[26] Other communities are close to 45 percent. If we weigh the percentages of Orthodox, Conservative, and Reform by the total Jewish population of each community (excluding Los Angeles, where the distribution still appears to be in a state of flux), we find that 15 percent of the Jews identify themselves as Orthodox, 26 percent as Reform, and 47 percent as Conservative. However, we are dealing here only with communities whose combined Jewish population is less than 10 percent of the total Jewish population of the United States.

In its infancy, the Conservative movement (with some exceptions) represented an upper-class formulation of elitist traditional Judaism. But its synagogues were more adaptable to the changing needs of American Jews than were those of Orthodoxy. Some Conservative rabbis were themselves in the forefront of those clamoring for change. But the changes which the rabbis sought were rooted in ideological convictions about the nature of Judaism. The masses sought change for very different reasons.

The alliance between the masses of East European immigrants or their descendants and the Conservative movement finally took place as the East Europeans abandoned the traditional folk religion of Orthodoxy and sought new forms of Jewish expression. Conservatism became predominant in areas of "third settlement." This was the most fashionable ethnic settlement and typically was located near the city limits, where residence "symbolized the attainment of solid middle-class position

or better and is indicative of a relatively high level of acculturation."[27] Here Jews constituted a distinct minority of the population and were surrounded, not by other ethnic groups over
whom they might feel a sense of status superiority, but rather
by Protestants and "old Americans" to whom they were subordinate in status. "The importation of the Orthodox synagogue
to areas of third settlement would not have helped to reduce
this status hiatus; it would in fact only have served to underline
it."[28]

It is not surprising, then, that Jews sought to develop a new
form of worship. The surprise is that Conservative synagogues
still conformed so closely to traditional Orthodoxy. The content
was not changed because the new Conservative Jews had no
interest in content. They were folk traditionalists or "re-
formed" secularists with a communal or ethnic definition of
Judaism. They were quite concerned with group survival, not
very interested in religion, and in search of institutions which
expressed values of both communal survival and integration or
acculturation to middle-class American standards.

To the upwardly mobile, status-conscious, economically successful East European Jews of the second or even first generation, there was a tremendous socioeconomic cost in being Orthodox. The economic cost came from not working on the
Sabbath and the holidays. A social-status cost resulted from affiliation with an institution lacking in decorum, unconcerned
with physical amenities, and chaotic in worship. There was an
intellectual cost in paying lip service to a faith burdened with
real and imagined superstition which was out of keeping with
the prevailing spirit of rationalism and secularism. Hence the
immigrant sought new institutional outlets for his Judaism.
These outlets had to be outwardly religious, since this was the
most legitimate expression of Judaism in America; but they also
had to provide a focus for expressing his essentially communal
concerns.

The growth of Conservatism in turn took the pressure off

Orthodoxy to accommodate itself rapidly to the American environment. Conservative Judaism provided a safety valve for discontented Orthodox Jews and reduced the demand for radical innovation within Orthodoxy, leaving it relatively unconcerned with integration. However, this also changed with the growth of an American-born rabbinate and laity.

Conservative Judaism is the primary Jewish expression of the East European immigrant and his descendants. It is fair to say that the folk religion of the contemporary American Jew is more adequately expressed through Conservatism than through any other movement. But it was not just shaped by the Jewish folk religion; it developed its own elite religion, its own ideology and practices which were shared by its leadership but not by the masses of Conservative Jews. In Conservatism, far more than in Orthodoxy or Reform, there is a sharp division between folk religion and elite religion. The original adherents of Orthodox folk religion have died out or become Conservative. Reform is experiencing a crisis in its own formulation. In fact, considerable numbers of Reform Jews, especially in the East, and many of its leaders share the folk religion of Conservative Judaism. Some nominally Orthodox Jews (though none of its leaders) also participate in the folk religion characteristic of Conservatism. Consider first, however, the elite religion of Conservative Judaism.

The Elite Religion of Conservative Judaism

Conservative Judaism traces its intellectual origin to the Historical School of Judaism in nineteenth-century Europe.[29] It represents a commitment to the historical traditions of Judaism, which it acknowledges as primarily legalistic and textual. Unlike Orthodoxy, however, Conservative Judaism sees the Jewish people and their history—through which God acts—as the source of authority, rather than the sacred texts—through which, according to the Orthodox, God speaks. Thus Conservative Judaism opens the theoretical possibility for reform and even radical change in Jewish law, depending upon how one interprets Jewish history and law, the needs of the time, and the mix between past and present authority. The elitist ideology of Conservatism is shared by most of the nine hundred or so members of the Rabbinical Assembly (the rabbinical arm of Conservatism) and by a few hundred, perhaps as many as a few thousand, Conservative educators and Jewishly literate laymen.

The center of Conservative Judaism for this small community of elite is the Jewish Theological Seminary (JTS). JTS is more traditional in orientation than even its elitist constituents, and its leaders have opposed the introduction of changes in Jewish law. This opposition has been generally successful (somewhat less so in the last few years), because the talmudic scholars who might introduce the changes or reforms with textual or legal justifications are on the JTS faculty and are generally the more traditional element within the Conservative movement.

But more significantly (for many Conservative rabbis would accept change even if it could not be legitimized by textual exegesis of some kind), JTS as an institution maintains a strong hold over its graduates and friends. This is due in part to the interpersonal relationships developed during student days between future rabbis and the JTS leadership, and in part to the enormous prestige of JTS as a center for scholarly research. In addition, many Conservative rabbis harbor feelings of guilt toward JTS. While this last point is highly speculative, it is based on the observation that many JTS graduates are disturbed by the kinds of compromises they have made with lay leaders of their congregations and feel that they have thereby betrayed the Seminary. Many Conservative rabbis have very ambivalent feelings toward JTS, to whom they relate as sons to a father. The same individuals who are willing to follow its leadership on matters of religious reform often express a sense of bitterness and even hostility toward the institution.

In recent years the faculty, curriculum, and standards of conduct within JTS have become even more traditional. This has produced some serious strains among the elite themselves, particularly between the rabbinical students and the JTS leadership. The problem is that JTS, whose students at one time came primarily from Orthodox homes, now recruits its students from homes where the prevailing atmosphere is Conservative folk religion. Before they come to JTS these students are socialized somewhat to the elite religion by the youth and camping movements of Conservatism. However, these institutions are staffed by individuals whose ideology is less traditional than that of the JTS leadership.

There is one central value, however, which is shared by both the elite religion and the folk religion of Conservatism: the value of integration into American life and a rejection of the notion that integration can only be sought at the expense of survival.

THE FOLK RELIGION OF AMERICAN JUDAISM (CONSERVATISM)

First- and second-generation American Jews of East European origin created the folk religion of American Judaism. Its adherents, as noted earlier, included virtually all the nominally Conservative Jews, many Reform, and some Orthodox.

Ritual of the Folk Religion

It is clear that the immigrant was willing to sacrifice a great deal that was basic and fundamental to the Jewish religion. He quickly denuded Judaism of much basic ritual. The laws of the Sabbath, kashrut, and family purity—the basic elements of Jewish ritual life—were abandoned by most of the first- and second-generation Jews. (Kosher-style, however, replaced kosher, a substitution which, as we noted, suggests that we are dealing with a choice for the sake of convenience, not a deliberate variation of life-style in an effort to conceal or lose one's identity.)

Despite the abandonment of the basic Jewish ritual, objections to intermarriage were retained. Why? Many of the early Reform rabbis raised no objections to intermarriage; indeed, they welcomed it. It is certainly consistent with Reform's definition of Judaism as a religion stressing morality and ethics which the Jew is obligated to diffuse among non-Jews. Why is intermarriage any more horrendous than violation of the Sabbath? In the catalog of ritual Jewish sins, there is hardly anything worse than desecration of the Sabbath. But obviously in the catalog of Jewish communal sins there is nothing worse than intermarriage. Countless Jewish mothers and fathers have cautioned their children before they left for college: "Forget Sabbath observance or kashrut if you must, but just make sure you don't fall in love with or marry a non-Jewish student." The proper ritual advice should be: "Marry a non-Jewish person if you must, but remember to observe the Sabbath." Of course, such advice sounds ludicrous. And the fact that it is ludicrous says something about the ritual, as opposed to communal, priorities of Jews.

The pattern of ritual which Jews have maintained is supportive of Jewish communalism and ethnicity, of the Jewish home and peoplehood. The seder, now celebrated as an annual festive family meal, is the most widely observed Jewish practice. The rites of passage—circumcision, bar mitzvah, a Jewish marriage, and a Jewish funeral—all serve to integrate the Jew into the community of fellow Jews. Hanukah was elaborated by American Jews to protect the child and to defend Judaism against the glamour and seductive power of Christmas. These holidays are the major points of contact between the Jew and his ritual traditions. Obviously, even these celebrations have undergone considerable distortion as they developed. The joyful and child-centered aspects were stressed and the more historically symbolic and existential theological aspects de-emphasized. Of somewhat lesser, though still considerable, importance is the celebration of the High Holy Days inaugurating the Jewish New Year. These days, Rosh Hashana and Yom Kippur, have acquired particular religious significance as memorials for departed parents and as the holidays of Jewish affirmation.

Some East European immigrants, forced by economic circumstances to work on the Sabbath, attended religious services in the early morning and then went to work. Second- and third-generation American Jews have reversed the process for the High Holy Days (the Sabbath is totally ignored). The folk religion enjoins the Jew from working on these days, regardless of whether he attends the synagogue or not and regardless of whether he prays or not. At least a token appearance at the synagogue is a desideratum, particularly at the time when memorial prayers for the dead are said. But the stress is not so much on prayer, and certainly not on hearing the shofar (the ram's horn blown on Rosh Hashana), which is central to the religious service. Rather, the stress is on staying away from work and thereby publicly acknowledging one's Jewish identity.

One does not have to believe with Émile Durkheim, the seminal French Jewish sociologist, that all religion is the celebration and ritualization of communal ties to observe that this is the major function of Jewish folk religion in America. It is not without significance that Mordecai Kaplan, whose philosophy of Reconstructionism was an effort to provide an ideological and elitist framework for Jewish folk religion, was influenced by Durkheim's theory of religion.

In a number of community studies, Jews were asked what they considered essential for a person to do in order to be a good Jew. The answer most frequently given was "Lead an ethical and moral life." Close behind and affirmed by over three-quarters of the respondents was "Accept his being a good Jew and not try to hide it."[30] Less than half, however, thought it was essential for one to belong to a synagogue or temple, and less than one-quarter thought that it was necessary to observe the dietary laws or attend weekly services in order to be considered a good Jew.

Associationalism

The Jewish folk religion includes a commitment to Israel (to be discussed in the next chapter) and to group survival, but its essence is one's social ties to other Jews. The distinguishing mark of American Jews is less and less how they behave and is certainly not what they believe; it is that they associate primarily with other Jews. Gerhard Lenski, in his Detroit area study, found that ties binding Jews to their religion are weaker than those of Protestants or Catholics, but ties binding them to one another are much stronger. More than other religious groups, "the great majority of Detroit Jews find most of their primary relationships within the Jewish subcommunity."[31] Even the highly acculturated and assimilated, wealthy, predominantly third-generation suburban American Jews studied by Sklare and Greenblum, continue to make their friends almost exclusively among other Jews.[32] They noted that "87 per cent of the parents had most or all of their close friendships with Jews, the same holds true for 89 per cent of our respondents."[33]

The reasons Jews themselves ascribe to this pattern are significant. By and large it is not a result of anti-Semitism or deliberate exclusion on the part of the non-Jews. Rather, many respondents emphasized:

Jews are predisposed to social contact and intimate association with other Jews because of a common religio-ethnic heritage and pervasive group identity. "It's because Jews go with Jews and Gentiles go with Gentiles. My background is so Jewish and my life is so Jewish that I'm happier surrounded by Jews," explains a young salesman's wife who is now active in Lilienthal Temple, although as an adolescent she had some close friends who were Gentile. "It's the identity, the background, the religion. It would be hard for a Gentile to be comfortable without these common bonds," elaborates an affluent lawyer and business executive who came to the United States from Russia when he was a youngster. . . . "There's a common notion of 'fate,' so we don't seek out non-Jews" is the concise reason given by a mother of three school-age children.

. . . A young businessman who observes almost none of the traditional religious practices to which he was exposed in childhood mentions similar reasons to account for the fact that he lost contact with the non-Jewish friends he had before marriage. "They went different paths because of differences in economics, education, and a different mode of living."[34]

As other Jews have noted, the major feature distinguishing Jews from non-Jews is the Jewish associational pattern.

The point I am trying to make is that, by and large, the Jews of America associate among themselves . . . they are culturally American, but socially in the ghetto. But, mind you, the ghetto is an American ghetto, not a Jewish ghetto. American Jews in B'nai B'rith . . . do precisely what other Americans do in the Knights of Columbus, the Rotarians . . . and other fraternal organizations. They do not differ in behavior patterns, in ritual, in professed ideals, in activities of all sorts, except for this one very significant thing, that they prefer to associate among themselves.[35]

Schools

Most Jewish parents who send their children to Jewish schools do so because they expect the school to serve those functions which the acculturated, Jewishly ignorant parent can no longer fulfill, "to reinforce Jewish identification through learning about Jewish history and traditions."[36] In his study of the growth of a new Jewish community, Herbert Gans notes that the community organized a school before a synagogue because the school was necessary as "an institution which transmits norms of ethnic culture and symbols of identification, whereas the home and the family are run by secular, middle-class behavior patterns."[37]

A synagogue bulletin carried the following argument by the principal of the congregation's supplementary Hebrew high school, urging parents to enroll their children:

Our adolescent youngster, for instance, begins to evaluate the Synagogue he once accepted unthinkingly. Does he really need worship or home observances? Does Jewish living do him or the world any good? Do Bible stories about tribes and miracles deserve all this fuss? These are really adolescent problems, not Jewish ones. If a child did not continue on to public high school, he would be assailed by the same doubts concerning the value of his secular elementary education. Such problems do not usually trouble a child who carries on his Jewish education through the high school level.

The writer's rationale for the child's continuing his Jewish education is worth noting. Jews traditionally educated their children in order to teach them how to live as good Jews. Now parents are urged to enroll their children so that the school may transmit to them the *value* of being Jewish.

The first generation of immigrants did not establish many Jewish schools. The reason, no doubt, was not only their preoccupation with economic survival and acculturation, but also the confidence in their own ability to transmit their communal ethnic identity to the next generation. However, this confidence was dissipated in the next generation as Jewish culture became attenuated. Jewish parents turned to the schools to socialize the Jewish child to the values of communality, ethnicity, and survival. Reform Judaism, seeking to transmit the principles of the *religion,* found the Sunday school sufficient. Even in the 1960s, 81 percent of the children in Reform Jewish schools attended one-day-a-week (primarily Sunday) schools.[38]

For the Conservatives this was not enough. Anxious to root the child in Jewish culture, they required at least a supplementary afternoon school, and since 1957 they have even organized a few of their own day schools. (Of course, the crucial role of the elitist leadership of the Conservative movement in this process cannot be underestimated.) Today 63 percent of all children in institutions under Conservative auspices attend Jewish schools two days a week or more; 58 percent, three days a week or more.[39] The Orthodox offer an even more intensive Jewish education.

Jewish education today is predominantly under synagogue auspices, a development consistent with the crucial role religion plays in legitimizing the Jewish desire for communal survival. By the same token, the specifically religious and cultic services which the synagogue provides are often secondary to its educational services. Parents are recruited as synagogue members when their child reaches the age of six, seven, or eight, and is ready for Jewish school. The education generally terminates at the age of thirteen, at which point the parents themselves may disaffiliate. In a 1965 survey of its congregational membership, the United Synagogue of America (Conservative Judaism's congregational organization) found that among 422 synagogues reporting, 33,734 families had joined in the last three years; and among 398 congregations reporting, 21,826 families had disaffiliated. Where disaffiliation did not occur as a result of death or members moving out of the community, 48 percent reported disaffiliation because the son "had completed Bar Mitzvah or Hebrew School."[40]

The pattern of synagogue affiliation varying with the child's age is also suggested in a recent study of the Greater Boston Jewish community.[41] The study found that synagogue membership increased from 24 percent of Jews in the 21–29 age group to 55 percent for the 30–39 group, 65 percent for ages 40–49, and then fell to 59 percent for those 50–64. One must consider the fact that the older Jew is more likely to be an immigrant and hence both more likely to consider himself Orthodox and more likely to affiliate with a synagogue.[42] This suggests that, where nativity and religious preference are constant (that is, if we considered only second- or third-generation Conservative

Jews), we would be likely to find a sharp drop in synagogue affiliation after the age of 50.

The Synagogue

The synagogue plays a crucial role in the folk religion of the Jews. Statistics are difficult to ascertain, but the combined estimates of members of all Orthodox, Conservative, and Reform congregations suggest that about 60 percent of American Jews are affiliated with a synagogue. According to the most recent community surveys, less than 20 percent of the Jews reported attending synagogue services oftener than once a month.[43]

But the synagogue is far more than a religious center. It tends to be the center for all Jewish activity. Sixty-six percent of the respondents in the Boston survey thought that this is what a synagogue should be.[44] It provides recreational and educational facilities, lectures and art classes, social outlets, golden age clubs, and a meeting place for other nonsynagogal Jewish organizations in the area. It raises funds not only for its own needs but for Jewish philanthropic purposes as well. The synagogue-based campaign provides a major source of funds for federations of Jewish philanthropies and for assistance to Jews abroad, particularly in Israel. Furthermore, secular Jewish organizations such as B'nai B'rith and the American Jewish Congress are not alternatives to the synagogue. Most members of the major Jewish communal organizations are synagogue members. Indeed, Jewish organizational membership tends to be a supplement rather than an alternative. Those who are affiliated with Jewish organizations are most likely to identify themselves with the religious community. According to Bernard Lazerwitz, "the two dominating factors of Jewish identification which are also strongly associated with one another are the religio-pietistic and Jewish organizational factors."[45]

The synagogue is the institutional center of Jewish life. Its public image is religious, its ostensible director is a clergyman, and its activity is therefore legitimate. The official ideology of the synagogue and the rabbi is that of an elite religion, but its content is that of the Jewish folk religion.

Reconstructionism

There was one effort, characteristically arising out of the Conservative movement, to reformulate the essence of American Jewish folk religion in ideological terms, and hence to institutionalize it and provide it with a formal leadership. This was the Reconstructionist philosophy and movement founded by Mordecai Kaplan in the 1920s. Kaplan's major work is *Judaism as a Civilization: Toward a Reconstruction of American-Jewish Life,* a title which suggests both a traditional view of Judaism and at the same time its reformulation in contemporary terminology.[46] The Reconstructionists challenged the notion of God as a Being. They redefined Him as a power and force in man and nature which makes for salvation, by which they mean freedom, justice, love, truth, and creativity. Under the influence of Durkheim and Dewey, Kaplan sought to explicate or make manifest in religion what others had seen as its latent function: social solidarity and the strengthening of peoplehood. Kaplan sought to retain the form of many traditional observances by reinvesting them with contemporary humanist meaning or national-historical significance.

The most remarkable feature of Reconstructionism is its failure as an institutionalized movement. Kaplan taught at the Jewish Theological Seminary from 1909 to 1963, serving also as dean of its Teachers Institute. He was a very popular teacher and for many years the most influential instructor there. Two generations of Conservative rabbis and educators came under Kaplan's influence. Since 1934 the Jewish Reconstructionist Foundation has published a lively biweekly periodical, *The Reconstructionist,* which has attracted many outstanding Jewish intellectuals as contributors and subscribers. And yet Reconstructionism has made few inroads into organized Jewish life. Only a handful of synagogues are associated with it, it has little money, and since the 1950s it has failed to gain the affection of young intellectuals, particularly within the Conservative movement.

Kaplan was not saying anything very new. He articulated in a provocative and intellectual manner the folk religion of American Jews. Why did his movement strike such a small chord if most Jews consciously or unconsciously are really Reconstructionists? The answer rests in the fact that to label one's religion explicitly as Reconstructionism is to identify it as a sham. Jews have preferred to deceive themselves and others about the nature of their faith and commitment. For the intellectuals of the 1930s, Reconstructionism had a more positive image. The Jewish Theological Seminary student, for example, knew he had lost the traditional Jewish faith in God and belief in the divine authority of religious law. Coming as he generally did from an Orthodox home and attending an institution of Conservative Judaism, he was quite self-conscious about his divergence from tradition. But he did not want to break with Judaism. He not only wanted to remain Jewish but to believe that he could function as a rabbi within the traditional Jewish fold. Kaplan offered him a rationale and a justification. Reconstructionism had an appeal to Jewish intellectuals, particularly rabbis, as long as there were young men who wanted to be rabbis and didn't want to be—or found they couldn't be—"religious." But the number of such young men, particularly in the Conservative rabbinate, is declining.

The institutional weakness of Reconstructionism lies partly in the fact that if one wants to be Jewish and not religious, there are secular Jewish organizations which can occupy one's energy and attention. Jewish philanthropic organizations, Zionist organizations, B'nai B'rith, the American Jewish Congress, the American Jewish Committee, and other groups provide outlets for one's Jewish identification outside a religious context. These secular Jewish organizations tend to specialize in one aspect of

Jewish life or to concentrate on one type of Jewish problem. But they maintain secondary activities in the hope of appealing to all Jews, regardless of their particular interest.

Pure Jewish secularism has no legitimacy in America (witness the demise of Jewish secularist labor and Yiddishist schools, and the inability of Zionists to establish a network of schools, as they have done in a number of other countries). Consequently, the secular organizations themselves have increasingly incorporated religion into the structure of their activity. They generally have one or more rabbis on their staffs, they often introduce some minor religious service into their meetings or conferences, and they articulate their special interests—whether they be Jewish-Christian relations, defense against real or imagined anti-Semitism, support for Israel, or even battling for strict separation of church and state—in quasi-religious terminology. Thus even Jewish secular organizations are "religious." Many spokesmen for these organizations deny that they are secular. To many Jews they differ from Orthodox, Conservative, and Reform synagogues only in their nondenominationalism.

A second factor which has handicapped Reconstructionism is the increased "religiousness" of the American Jew. We have suggested all along that religion is the public façade for the essentially communal content of Jewish identification. But as Jews become increasingly acculturated they take the façade of their public image more seriously. This is the paradoxical result of the fact that more and more Jews learn about themselves from the outside world, particularly the mass media. Newspapers, magazines, and television are probably the primary sources of information for Jews about Judaism. But the mass media obtain their information from the façade of Jewish life, not from the inner content.

A good illustration of the paradox is reflected in the development of the Synagogue Council of America. This organization is composed of representatives from the rabbinical and congregational bodies of all three denominations. The Synagogue

Council was a necessary creation if Judaism was to speak with one voice on religious matters. Its spokesmen are the public representatives of Judaism on matters of religious concern. At one time the Synagogue Council was a paper organization which neither Orthodoxy, Conservatism, nor Reform took seriously. But once the *New York Times* and *Time* magazine began treating it as the Jewish counterpart of the National Council of Churches, and once the Protestants and Catholics took it seriously, it became a serious organization in the minds of many Jews and its importance began to escalate.

The process of acculturation has led an increasing number of Jews to believe that Judaism is a religion. Consequently, if Jews are nonreligious, they more readily lose a sense of Jewish identification. But if they desire a continuing identification, they must be religious. For such Jews, God must be more than the impersonal force or power that Reconstructionism asserts.

Reconstructionism, then, has lost much of its appeal for Conservative Jews, particularly rabbinical students. These young men now come from Conservative backgrounds. They never broke with Orthodoxy; they have no nostalgia for replicas of East European life-styles, no guilt feelings about their religious beliefs or behavior. Furthermore, they are not attracted to the rabbinate by a depression economy which offers no occupational alternatives. They want to become rabbis because they believe Judaism has something to say of religious and social significance.

Reconstructionism has enjoyed some increase in popularity, however, among Reform Jews, though not among its theological spokesmen. Reform theologians either are far more committed to religious existentialism and belief in a personal God or, at the other extreme, are far more radical than Kaplan. The radical Reform Jews deny the utility of the God concept or the existence of a meaningful Jewish tradition. Nevertheless, Reform, like every other American Jewish institution, was engulfed by the East European immigrant. This was not only true among the laity but also among the Reform rabbinate, and resulted in the introduction of more traditional symbols among the Reform, a greater emphasis on traditional observance, and greater sympathy toward Zionism. David Philipson, a member of the first graduating class of Hebrew Union College in 1883, viewed these developments at the 1931 meetings of the Reform rabbis with chagrin, and attributed them to "the large number of young rabbis who come from Zionistic and Orthodox environments."[47]

As Reform found an East European Jewish identity, Kaplan's notion of peoplehood and his justification of many ritual practices as folkways had special resonance for some. In a recent survey of first- and last-year students at rabbinical seminaries, respondents were asked to check the name of an individual who best reflected their religious, philosophical, or theological position.[48] Between the first and the last year, the number of Jewish Theological Seminary students choosing Kaplan decreased, but at the Reform schools the number increased. To many Reform Jews of East European background, classical Reform Judaism appears schismatic. For them, Kaplan represents the route back to the unity of the Jewish people.

CONSEQUENCES OF THE GROWTH OF "RELIGIOUS" JUDAISM

The increasingly religious definition of Judaism has had a number of important consequences for the institutional structure of American Jewish life. One has been to strengthen the influence of Orthodox Judaism. Another has been in the relationship between folk and elite Judaism.

Development of Orthodox Judaism

Orthodox Judaism was the original folk religion of the East European immigrant. The more successful immigrants and their descendants abandoned Orthodoxy as too old-worldly. What really happened was that the bearers of the folk religion became more acculturated and found a more congenial home within Conservative Judaism. Orthodoxy did not disappear, however, although it seemed for a time that it might.

Orthodoxy kept the loyalty of the less successful, elderly, and unacculturated Jews, and of those few Jews who were attracted by its elitist content. Some second-generation or younger immigrants were Americanized but remained religiously traditional for personal or familistic reasons. The Young Israel movement emerged out of this latter group, which also provided the constituency for the few large middle- and upper-middle-class Orthodox synagogues that are associated today with what is sometimes called modern Orthodoxy.[49] The rabbinical leadership for the modern Orthodox came primarily from the graduates of the Rabbi Isaac Elchanan Theological Seminary of Yeshiva University.

Those more rooted in the folk traditions of Eastern Europe, led by rabbis of East European training who were organized in the Union of Orthodox Rabbis, viewed the graduates of Yeshiva and their organization, the Rabbinical Council of America, as insufficiently religious. They denigrated the Yeshiva graduates, despite the fact that many members of the Union of Orthodox Rabbis were parties to the grossest violations of Jewish law, most notably the granting of rabbinical approval to food products that were of questionable kashrut. It is undeniably true that many "modern Orthodox" rabbis compromised religious principle in certain areas of Jewish life, or, if you will, made concessions to certain contemporary standards and mores of their congregations. But by any standard of religious practices, their personal and organizational conduct was less reprehensible than that of many older East European rabbis who served as members in good standing in the Union of Orthodox Rabbis. Nevertheless, the cultural orientation of the latter was so pervasive and so interrelated to their religious outlook that any English-speaking, clean-shaven Jew in modern dress was immediately considered somewhat irreligious.

Orthodoxy probably could not have survived if it had had to depend on modern Orthodoxy and the few remaining Sephardic congregations alone. However, it was renewed in the 1930s and 1940s by new immigration. Those years before and immediately after the Second World War brought to the United States an influx of Orthodox immigrants far more militant than those who had come earlier. They found an Orthodox community under the leadership of rabbis who seemed in despair about the future of Orthodoxy and convinced of the necessity for compromise. They found institutions such as the supervision of kashrut in the hands of people whom they considered unreliable or careless. They found a bare handful of day schools and Yeshiva University and the Rabbinical Council of America ready to accommodate themselves to secular culture. They found almost no institutions with total commitment to the traditional Torah life which had been their world. And, unlike the earlier immigrants, they were the bearers of an elitist religion. Their traditionalism was textual rather than communal. Their first collective action was the establishment of yeshivot, schools for the advanced study of the Talmud.

In 1941 Rabbi Aaron Kotler, famous as a talmudic scholar and Orthodox leader in Eastern Europe, arrived in the United States intending to spend a short time and then move on to Palestine. A handful of Orthodox Jews persuaded him to stay in the United States to build Torah institutions. Reb Aharon, as he was known in the Orthodox world, assembled twenty students, mostly graduates of American yeshivot, some already ordained as rabbis, and established the Beth Medrash Govoha of America in Lakewood, New Jersey, now also known as the Rabbi Aaron Kotler Institute for Advanced Learning. His choice of site was a deliberate attempt to isolate his students from American life and facilitate total concentration on the study of the Talmud. Within a few years he was joined by some former students from

Europe; by 1946 registration had risen to one hundred, and by 1970 to over three hundred.

Reb Aharon's conviction was that Torah could grow and be "experienced" in America only through *lernen* ("learning" in the parlance of the Orthodox world), studying Talmud. According to one of Reb Aharon's former students, only "sharing the experience of the halakhic process [the formulating of law] could enable the Jew to understand the heartbeat of Judaism." The student at Lakewood lived on a small subvention from the yeshiva and whatever other financial help he got from his family or wife. Students sat and learned for as long as they wished. When they felt ready to leave, they left. Many of these students became teachers of Talmud and went on to found or reshape institutions in the Lakewood pattern. But few graduates of this institution or similar ones became congregational rabbis.

Reb Aharon himself did not confine his activity to Lakewood. He engaged in a multitude of activities which gained recognition for his point of view. Besides his activity and leadership of institutions and movements in Israel which reflected his point of view, he also served as chairman of the rabbinical administrative board of Torah Umesorah, the National Society for Hebrew Day Schools in the United States. Despite the shortage of trained teachers and administrators, the number of all Hebrew elementary and secondary schools under Orthodox auspices has grown from forty-five to over three hundred in the last twenty-five years. Reb Aharon elicited tremendous passion and dedication from those with whom he came in contact. He brooked no compromise nor did he ever question or seem to doubt his own path. He was a particularly charismatic leader.

The heart of this Orthodox world which Reb Aharon and others like him shaped are the post-high school yeshivot, except Yeshiva University and the Hebrew Theological College in Skokie, Illinois. There are today probably close to ten thousand men studying the Talmud intensively at yeshivot on a post-high school level. Many are older students, some of them married, who spend the entire day studying the Talmud while receiving a small subvention from the school. Many of these students have already been ordained; many others have no intention of obtaining a rabbinical degree, which, in fact, has a practical value only if one plans to become a practicing rabbi. (Many heads of European yeshivot never had semikah, rabbinical ordination, which is simply a certificate attesting to one's competence in deciding questions of Jewish law. A scholar of renown needed no such certificate. The very process of learning Talmud is a raison d'être and way of life to these men, who eventually will themselves become heads of yeshivot and teachers of Talmud.)

Graduates of these schools provide the major source of staff for the day-school movement. Many, including those with ordination, avoid the rabbinate because they neither wish nor are able to serve predominantly nonobservant Orthodox memberships. By choice or absence of alternatives, they enter the less prestigious and more poorly paid field of Jewish education or engage in a secular occupation.

Among the Orthodox immigrants were a number of Hasidic leaders and disciples. The best known of these groups are the Lubavitcher and Satmar Hasidim. Although many of the Hasidim, whose Judaism has a greater folk orientation, cling tenaciously to some of their special customs—even retaining their traditional East European dress—they are generally indistinguishable ideologically from the Orthodox yeshiva world. They differ only in their loyalty to their rebbe, a Hasidic leader to whom the followers attribute extraordinary qualities and around whom they cluster.

The increasingly religious definition of Judaism has strengthened Orthodoxy in many ways. It has given it greater legitimacy within the Jewish community. Judaism has always known of the nonobservant Jew who might be quite indifferent to any ritual and belief but who, having been raised in an Orthodox environment, finds nostalgic satisfaction in attendance at familiar synagogue services once or twice a year. To him, as to his coreligionist at the other end of the spectrum, Orthodoxy is "more religious" than Conservatism or Reform.

But Orthodoxy is particularly favored in an era in which religion has gained not only respectability but even intellectual recognition. In a period in which affirmation of supernaturalism is no longer a cause for embarrassment, and where one prevailing mood among the intellectual avant-garde is to stress individual and personal religious experience of a nonrational nature, Orthodoxy finds a receptive ear. It is a time when a Reform rabbi, writing with a tinge of envy and much sympathy about ultrareligious Hasidic groups, barely conceals his disdain for his own congregants. In this atmosphere a Jew, particularly if he is middle class, gains a certain status among Jewishly alert groups through affiliation with an Orthodox congregation. This status is inversely related to the degree to which the Orthodox congregation modernizes its services, grows in membership, and emulates the Conservative and Reform synagogues in the variety of nonsacred activities offered to the membership.

The large size of the Conservative and Reform synagogues propels some Jews to seek alternatives in Orthodoxy. No matter how artfully constructed, the physical plant that is intended to seat a thousand or more worshipers, educate hundreds of children, and provide social and recreational activities for an entire neighborhood, while it may be inspiring and attractive to most people, will be forbidding to at least a few. The lack of warmth and the anonymity of the large Reform and Conservative congregations suffer by contrast with the intimate feeling of community evoked by small Orthodox synagogues, independent of belief or disbelief in credal Orthodoxy.

There is also the phenomenon of Yavneh, a growing organization of Orthodox college youth, some of whose members come from nonreligious homes and therefore turn to Orthodoxy to seek a strong Jewish religious identity.

None of the foregoing should suggest that Orthodoxy is growing numerically. It is probably declining in absolute numbers and will in all likelihood continue to decline, given the disproportionate number of older Jews who are nominally Orthodox. What is happening, however, is that Orthodoxy's elitist elements are being strengthened as its folk elements disappear. In addition, for the first time Orthodoxy is not only relatively successful in keeping its own young people, but also offers some attraction to the non-Orthodox. The magnitude of this attraction should not be exaggerated. The significant factor is that it exists at all.

Religious Elitism and the Growth of Jewish Denominationalism

The religious definition of Judaism strengthens elitist religion within Conservativism and Reform as well as within Orthodoxy. Within Orthodoxy, the religious right wing and the talmudic scholars—those most at home in the sacred textual tradition and those, therefore, with the greatest stake in the present system of religious authority—have assumed the leadership. In Conservatism and Reform, the influence of the rabbi, the bearer of their elitist religion, has been enhanced because only the rabbi has the requisite knowledge and "authority" to manipulate the symbols of the religion and organize its cult. Of course, this notion of rabbinic authority was borrowed from Christianity by the modern Jew, who, religious though he may be, tends increasingly to be religious in a Christian rather than in a traditional Jewish sense.

One result of the growth of elitism has been the development of Jewish denominationalism. Religious denominationalism among Protestants has often been associated with differences in social class. It might be well to explore the question of social change and question whether certain Jewish religious developments might not be ascribed more properly to change in social conditions.

The identification of individual Jews with Orthodoxy, Conservatism, and Reform in America is indeed associated with differential social characteristics. In view of the fact that a substantial segment of all three denominations shares in the Jewish folk religion, one might even argue that social and life-style differences have been the major source of differentiation among the denominations. Reform Jews were the wealthiest and best educated, Orthodox the poorest and least educated; indeed, many of the ritual and behavioral differences between Orthodoxy and Reform do reflect differences in social class. (Since Orthodox Jews tend to be older than other Jews and of more recent immigration, they are naturally the poorest and least educated. Whether differences in the social characteristics of the denominations will remain the same in the future is problematical.)

But if the major distinguishing features of the three Jewish branches are their social characteristics, then one might anticipate a lessening of Jewish denominationalism and perhaps even a merging of the three groups should their members become socially homogeneous. This is, after all, the process that has taken place among Protestants. Jews who rise in social class might simply leave one denomination, Orthodoxy, and switch their affiliation to Conservative or Reform. This unquestionably has happened. But the experience of Protestantism has been that not all members of a lower-status denomination change to a higher-status one as they rise in social class. Instead, whole groups or denominations tend to respond to changes in their members' social status by changes in their prescribed religious practices and beliefs. These changes help account for the growing ecumenism among Protestants.[50]

In order to examine changes in the social characteristics of Orthodox, Conservative, and Reform Jews, synagogues in the Greater New York area were examined during two periods: 1948–1952 and 1958–1962.[51] Synagogues were located by census tract, and the median income of the residents of each tract was examined. The assumption was that a new synagogue reflected the social characteristics of the area in which it was located, and that the relative class composition of Jews was proportional to that of the other residents within a given census tract. The study found that, on the average, Reform Jews have been and continue to be in the highest income bracket, Orthodox Jews in the lowest, and Conservative Jews between the two but closer to Reform. However, since the Second World War the overlap between the three groups is considerable. Reform Judaism is no longer confined to Jews of the highest income and Orthodoxy to those of the lowest. Instead, the social distance among Orthodox Jews themselves, or Conservatives, or Reform Jews, is growing. In other words, a growing number of Orthodox synagogues are now located in areas whose social characteristics are above those of some Conservative and Reform synagogues.

This overlapping may in the long run lead to increased cooperation between the three groups. But it is dangerous to make such a prediction without taking into account the growth of elite religion. Jews who share a folk religion may readily move from one denomination to another if the distinctions are based only on acculturation, style, and taste. But should elite religion continue to develop more rapidly than changes in the class composition of the three groups, there is no reason to believe that social homogeneity would inevitably lead to religious unity. In fact, Orthodoxy, which has the most highly developed elitist leadership and which has been most successful in repressing its folk elements (partly because its adherents of the folk element abandoned Orthodoxy for Conservatism), has become more sectarian with its rise in social status. The elite religion of Orthodoxy must be more sectarian than the folk religion because communal consensus carries much less weight in its scale of values. The increase in income among Orthodox Jews has simply meant that its elite leadership now has greater resources and is better able to strike out on an independent path from Conservatism and Reform.

Conservative and Reform leaders in turn have sought to delineate the particular boundaries differentiating their own groups from Orthodoxy. In part this has been a response to Orthodoxy's denial of their religious legitimacy in a period when religious legitimacy is increasingly important. In part it has been a response to the threat posed by the synagogues' peripheral nonworship activity which engulfs the religious center and reduces the rabbis' authoritative platform. This threat has always existed and has been an inherently unsatisfactory condition for the rabbi, who is now in a position to fight back. But most of all, the Conservative and Reform leaders have had to define their particular boundaries in response to the increasing sense of religious (as distinct from communal) Jewish identity among many young people. This identity requires that the rabbi assert a religious definition of his own denomination if his synagogue is to have any meaning.

But once boundaries are asserted in elitist terms, differences between the groups become significant. The folk religion also distinguished between Orthodoxy, Conservatism, and Reform —Reform being modern, Orthodoxy old-worldly, and Conservatism between the two. To the third- or fourth-generation American Jews, to whom the conflict over acculturation is a fight long past and for whom Judaism is a religion, these distinctions are trivial and hardly enough to sustain or justify independent religious establishments. The elitist distinctions in theology and practice appear to be of greater substance. In their efforts to impose elitist definitions on the masses of synagogue members, each group has paid increased attention to the development of synagogue-based youth groups and summer camps. Part of the impetus was to recruit young men for the elite ranks, particularly the rabbinate, but the enterprise can also be seen as an effort on the part of each movement to socialize the future synagogue members to the values and definitions of the elite.

PROSPECTS FOR THE FUTURE

The self-definition of Judaism in religious rather than communal-ethnic terms has been a major tendency in American Jewish life. But there are forces operating against this trend which might well become dominant in the future. These include the decline of Christian churches and the deterioration of organized religion's reputation, which may result in Jews being more comfortable with a different structural façade. In addition, there is the increasing significance of the role of Israel in the life of the American Jew, and the Jewish identity which is aroused by threats to Israel's safety. Support for and interest in Israel by some Jews represents a secular and ethnic outlet for Jewish expression which is not necessarily religious in nature. Should there be increasing manifestations of anti-Semitism in the United States, Jews will be drawn together across denominational lines. Anti-Semitism, like perils to Israel, will activate religiously uninterested Jews who might otherwise have left the community. However, the question is: What does Israel represent for most Jews?

4

AMERICAN JEWS AND ISRAEL

We have noted that a religious self-definition has maximized attainment of the two core values of American Jews: integration and survival. But how is one to explain the importance that Israel plays in American Jewish life, particularly in the last few years? Doesn't the obvious attachment of American Jews to Israel, to its survival and even more to its symbols, contradict our assertion about Jewish self-definition as a religion? Is it not possible that the increasing importance of Israel in American Jewish life presages a changing self-definition in which the ethical-national may replace the religious?

The thrust of this chapter is that Israel has not replaced religion as the focus of Jewish identity; rather, it has increasingly become the content or the expression of Jewish religious identity.

ISRAEL'S IMPORTANCE TO AMERICAN JEWS

While one must generalize with caution about the New Left, it seems that most of its leading journals and most of its leading spokesmen are either hostile to Israel or neutral in the Arab-Israeli conflict. The fact that so many Jewish youths are to be found in the New Left is evidence that not all Jews support

Israel. But then not all Jews share any characteristic which we have attributed to American Judaism in the previous chapters. We noted, for example, that American Judaism was synagogue-centered, yet we estimated that only 60 percent of American Jews were affiliated with a synagogue (a figure which doesn't take into account the low rate of affiliation among specialized groups such as people of college age, the unmarried, and probably the elderly). In other words, there is a sizable group, perhaps 25 to 30 percent of American Jews, who stand either outside or on the margins of the community and to whom many of the generalizations made here do not apply. Some of them are so close to assimilation that they no longer feel ties to anything Jewish. Others are self-haters or are in conscious rebellion against the community, so that they automatically oppose whatever the community favors. But to the overwhelming majority of American Jews, including even many from this marginal and alienated group of Jews, Israel is of great importance.

Quantitative indicators do not adequately measure the importance of Israel to American Jewry or, for that matter, its greatly increased importance since May 1967, the period immediately preceding the Six-Day War. Since then virtually the entire American Jewish community has been engulfed by concern for Israel. We may easily forget, for example, that in interviews of upper-middle-class Jews in suburban Lakeville conducted just ten years prior to the Six-Day War, only 21 percent of the sample thought that in order to be a good Jew it was *essential* that one support Israel. Forty-seven percent thought it was *desirable* though not essential, and 32 percent thought it had no bearing on whether or not one was considered a good Jew.[1] While we have no comparable study after 1967, every indication is that a much higher percentage would now say that in order to be a good Jew, support for Israel is essential, or at least desirable.

The best single measure may be the financial contributions of American Jews to Israel, as shown in the accompanying table.

As the figures clearly demonstrate, 1967 was a turning point in American Jewish attitudes toward Israel, at least insofar as attitudes were expressed in financial contributions to Israel.

Philanthropic contributions are only one indicator of Israel's importance today and its increasing importance over the last few years. A more significant indicator is Israel's symbolic importance to American Jews. The flag of Israel, the Israeli national anthem, and art objects from Israel, sanctified because they come from Israel, have assumed religious or quasi-religious meaning to an increasing number of American Jews.

If one could present graphically the time-space dimensions of the typical American Jew, it is obvious that only a small fraction of his time would be devoted to Jewish activity. Indeed, most of the time he probably would not even be self-consciously Jewish. But unquestionably one would also find that an increasing portion of that fraction of Jewish time-space, perhaps even most of it, is devoted to activity and thought surrounding Israel. This includes both time spent in attendance at meetings and rallies (minimal for most Jews), and conversation about Israel, reading or hearing news about Israel, and, most significantly in the last few years, trips to Israel.

Jewish educational institutions, from Sunday schools to day schools, devote increasing amounts of time to Israel, and there is increasing concern among Jewish educators about curriculum-planning for Israel.

Jewish organizations spend an increasing proportion of their budgets and energies on Israel programs. They have learned that in order to attract and hold their memberships they must demonstrate a strong orientation to Israel. They organize tours to Israel and seek to develop some special kind of program or activity in Israel; their professional executives spend more and more time in planning and consultation with other Jewish organizations on domestic political activity in Israel's behalf and in mobilizing their own membership for demonstrations of one kind or another in support of Israel.

Support for Israel, more than any single issue, represents a

TABLE 4.1   Contributions to UJA (Pledges) and Sale of Israel Bonds in the U.S.A.*

Year	UJA Pledges† ($ thousands)		Bond Sales
1948	150,000		
1949	103,000	est.	
1950	88,000	est.	
1951	80,100	(cash)	52,506
1952	69,800		46,516
1953	65,000		31,551
1954	60,000	est.	34,361
1955	60,000	est.	36,681
1956	75,000		45,699
1957	82,000		40,696
1958	68,000		37,763
1959	73,000		42,628
1960	61,000		41,390
1961	60,000		45,287
1962	63,500		46,396
1963	62,000		55,500
1964	59,600		70,356
1965	62,400		76,656
1966	64,400		76,176
1967	240,100		189,967
1968	149,700		107,019
1969	173,000		131,701
1970	202,000		176,000

*This table presents only the most readily available data on contributions to the United Jewish Appeal and sale of Israel Bonds in the United States.
SOURCE: *American Jewish Year Book*, vols. 55–71.
†Includes the Israel Emergency Fund but not the Israel Educational Fund.

boundary defining position in the communal consensus of American Jews. Every community (and the Jewish community is no exception) has some definition of deviance that is particular to it. In large measure it is the definition of deviance which defines the community, because it represents the manner in which the community distinguishes itself from the rest of society. Obviously, communities also differ in the controls and sanctions which they can exercise over deviant behavior. In the case of a voluntary community, such as the Jews in American society, the controls and sanctions are extralegal. They include moral sanctions, social sanctions, and, to a more limited extent, business and economic sanctions. (There are certain industries and certain communities where the Jews are so located and so organized that they can bring economic pressure to bear on each other.)

Support for Israel, as we have indicated, represents the crucial boundary today in the American Jewish community. It is inconceivable, for example, that any Jewish organization within the community (therefore this excludes the American Council of Judaism) would elect a leader who was opposed to Israel. I believe that a Jewish organization would more readily elect a leader who intermarried than one who opposed Israel. Indeed, as important as opposition to intermarriage still is as a definition of deviance and in boundary maintenance, it has in recent years receded in importance, whereas support for Israel has increased. In other words, most American Jews would probably view nonsupport of Israel as a greater "crime" for a Jew than the "crime" of intermarriage.

The bitterness which the Jewish community harbors to the New Left stems not from its revolution against the traditional morality upon which Jewish family life is based and without which, therefore, Judaism cannot survive; it does not even stem from its propensity to violence, which even Jews with only the most superficial sense of history recognize as a threat to Jewish security (Jews have always suffered in an atmosphere of violence even when the violence was not initially directed against them). Rather, the Jewish community is most bitter about the New Left because of its anti-Israel rhetoric. There are still substantial elements within the Jewish community who would like nothing better than the opportunity to embrace the New Left, to declare the harmony of its values with "prophetic justice," or traditional Jewish morality, but are dissuaded by the position of the New Left (or of its most significant elements) on the Israel-Arab encounter.

Having stressed Israel's importance in American Jewish life, we must now caution against exaggerating or, more correctly, misunderstanding the nature of its role. For purposes of another essay, a questionnaire was devised to probe the religious ideology of American Jewry and to find what ideological differences, if any, distinguish Orthodox, Conservative, and Reform Jews from each other and from Reconstructionists.[2] The questionnaire was mailed in late 1968 to 130 rabbinical leaders, including all executive committee members, of the Rabbinical Council of America (Orthodox rabbis), the Rabbinical Assembly of America (Conservative rabbis), and the Central Conference of American Rabbis (Reform rabbis). The response rate varied from 62 percent for the Orthodox to 90 percent for the Reform rabbis. In February 1969 the questionnaire was mailed to presidents of all synagogues affiliated with the Union of American Hebrew Congregations (Reform) or the United Synagogue of America (Conservative), and to the best available list of presidents whose synagogues were affiliated with the Union of Orthodox Jewish Congregations of America (Orthodox). In addition, the questionnaire was mailed to all chapter presidents of a certain large nondenominational Jewish organization. Since that organization requested anonymity, we will refer to it as NJO (National Jewish Organization). The rate of return to this mailing from NJO and Conservative and Reform presidents ranged from 38 to 42 percent, a satisfactory rate of return for a mailed questionnaire with no follow-up. Only 18 percent of the Orthodox synagogue presidents responded.

Some of the items included in the questionnaire pertained to Israel. They appeared in the form of statements with which respondents were asked to agree or disagree. All groups except Orthodox rabbis disagreed with the statement that "a Jew who really wants to do what Judaism requires of him should move to Israel." On the other hand, only the rabbis and laymen of the Reform disagreed with the statement that "Israel should become the spiritual center of world Jewry." For our purposes, however, the most interesting response was to the statement that "while there must be a warm fraternal relation between Jews of the U.S. and Israel, the center of American Jewish life must be *American* Judaism rather than a Jewish culture which has developed or will develop in the State of Israel" (italics appear in the original). Only the Orthodox rabbis and lay leaders disagreed with this statement. In other words, not only do American Jews deny *aliyah* (settlement in Israel) as a preeminent Jewish value, they do not really see Israel as an ideological or cultural center for themselves. We suggest that Israel, for all its importance, is not a spiritual, cultural, or ideological center for American Jews. Rather, concern for Israel, efforts in its behalf, and the symbols of Israel increasingly represent the content of American Judaism. Israel has become the major focus of Jewish expression, and therefore marks as deviant any Jew who opposes it.

Israel's increasing importance and special role in Jewish life is the result not only of factors which have directly escalated its significance, but also of factors which have reduced the importance of other focuses of Jewish expression. Let us consider the latter first.

FOCUSES OF JEWISH EXPRESSION

We have repeatedly stressed the significance of religion and the synagogue in American Jewish life. What we have left unanswered is what function religion or the synagogue serves. To put it another way: What does Jewish identity mean to the American Jew? To say that Jewish identity represents religious affiliation or even synagogue membership may be true, but it begs the question: What does being Jewish mean? Granted, it has something to do with being of a certain religion. But what does it mean to be of the Jewish religion?

The question has an ontological dimension to which we do not pretend to know the answer. "To feel Jewish means to feel *Jewish*" may be the best answer we can give. But there is another dimension to the question: How does the American Jew rationalize his feeling Jewish? How does the American Jew justify and legitimize the fact that he feels Jewish, that he acts out of a sense of identity with other Jews, or even that he continues to call himself a Jew? This is a question which the Jew must answer, however indirectly, to non-Jews, to other Jews, to his children, but perhaps most of all to himself.

Obviously, there are those who might answer the question in national or cultural terms, without reference to religion. Such individuals, however, represent a distinct minority of American Jews. We are concerned here with various focuses of Jewish expression, the various meanings of Jewish identity which can, in one way or another, be fitted into a religious conception of Judaism.

Anti-Semitism

One group, whose self-definition of Judaism stands on the margins of a religious conception of Judaism, are those to whom Judaism means defense against anti-Semitism. Only among the most marginal elements of the community is the fight against anti-Semitism the preeminent expression of Judaism. In other words, whereas virtually all Jews are sensitive to anti-Semitism, it is only the most marginal Jew who sees anti-Semitism as the force which binds him to the community. Ostensibly, such Jewish expression has little to to with religion, but in fact that is not the case. Synagogue affiliation or occasional synagogue attendance may be the manner in which the Jew demonstrates his own sense of pride in the face of anti-Semitism. This is particularly true since such types of Jews, more than any other, accept outgroup conceptions of what Judaism is. In addition, as one of its many activities the synagogue is alert to manifestations of anti-Semitism at the communal level and offers opportunities to oppose it.

Anti-Semitism undoubtedly provided a Jewish raison d'être

for many Jews during World War II and in the periods immediately preceding and following it. But it became far too frail a hook on which to hang one's Jewish identity in the late 1950s and early 1960s. Opinion surveys from that period showed a great decrease in anti-Semitic sentiment in the United States.[3] This decrease was accompanied by the opening of almost all doors in American society to the Jews. Jewish organizations which up till then had been preoccupied with fighting anti-Semitism branched out in their activities. By the mid-1950s anti-Semitism had so decreased in importance that it no longer provided a reasonable legitimation of Jewish identity or a focus of Jewish expression. The recurrence of anti-Semitism in the last few years from the New Left and from black militants does provide new opportunities, but significantly, a major expression of this anti-Semitism, at least in rhetoric, is in anti-Israel statements. Thus today, unlike the situation in the World War II period, the fight against anti-Semitism necessarily involves one with concern for Israel.

Prophetism—Social Justice

To many Jews, Judaism has meant the fight for social justice, civil rights, and civil liberties. The difficulty with this conception of Judaism is that on the surface it has very little to do with what is uniquely Jewish. One does not, after all, have to be Jewish to fight for Negro rights. But until the 1960s it was possible to believe that it helped. As we shall see in chapter 7, Jews are liberals, and it was Jewish organizations that were in the forefront of those very causes which liberals held so dear. Rabbis, especially Reform but many Conservative and even a handful of Orthodox rabbis, reminded their congregations of the special ties between Judaism and liberal causes, and of Jews' special responsibilities to the socially or economically underprivileged because they had themselves suffered so much injustice and were part of a "prophetic tradition." To many

Jews the statements "I am a Jew" and "I am a political liberal" were synonymous, and the Jewish tradition, Jewish ritual, and Jewish symbols were invested with social meaning.

By the mid-1960s, defining the meaning of Judaism as social justice had lost claims on reality. Jewish organizations had been replaced by black organizations or welfare organizations in the "prophetic" field. To be the most liberal was no longer to be the most radical, daring, bold, but rather to be the most cautious, the most middle-of-the-roadish. The stereotypical "political" clergyman was no longer a rabbi but a minister or, most recently, a priest. Most of those Jews who participated in the more radical political causes of the late 1960s viewed themselves as entirely divorced from Judaism. The middle-of-the-road Jewish liberal felt himself increasingly alienated from his traditional ideological concerns, so that social justice was no longer a satisfactory vehicle by which to define his focus of expression. Of course, a few members of the Jewish establishment have continued to maintain their old concerns and have continued to see in social justice a preeminent expression of Judaism,[4] but this is no longer a serious option for many Jews.

Peoplehood

To many Jews, Judaism was expressed in their interest in and concern for other Jews all over the world. Yet throughout the 1950s it seemed that the only Jews who really required care and concern—certainly the only group of Jews who aroused widespread interest—were those in Israel. In these days of rallies and demonstrations in behalf of Soviet Jewry, we easily forget that the overwhelming majority of American Jews and their leaders had lost all interest and concern with Soviet Jewry between the 1950s and mid-1960s. The Jews of the Arab countries, on the other hand, seemed so far removed and the sounds of their suffering so muted, the opportunities to help them so remote, that they too were outside the horizons of Jewish concern. Furthermore, American Jews had become deeply rooted in American culture, and the language and culture of Jews were so forgotten, that the sense of Jewish peoplehood inevitably faded. American Jews shared so much more with and felt so much more at home with non-Jewish Americans than with Jews of other countries that the sense of membership in an international people necessarily declined. This sense of peoplehood has in part been reawakened in the past few years. But it is really an outgrowth of the increased importance of Israel, of Israel's own sense of peoplehood, and in this sense concern for Israel is today more than anything else the uniting factor in Jewish identity.

Theology and Belief

Ritual observance has never been especially attractive to American Jews. But during the 1950s there was a revival of interest in theology associated with conceptions of religious existentialism. This interest ought not to be exaggerated. It did not touch any great emotional depths. It was a legitimate concern of a number of knowledgeable and thoughtful Jews, but other than that it represented an imitation of the theological interests and fads which were then current in the Christian world and were associated with a renewed interest in religion. It was this fad which made books with religious themes into best sellers and turned clergymen into TV personalities and the subjects of newspaper and magazine articles.

Given this widespread interest in the theological dimensions of religion (regardless of how shallow its bases might have been), it was possible for some American Jews in the 1950s and early 1960s to find a focus of Jewish expression or legitimize their sense of Jewish identity in questions of theology. Furthermore, it was among the theologians themselves that questions were raised about the centrality or signal importance of Israel in Jewish life. There was talk then of two centers, Israel and

America, just as once before there had been two centers of Jewish life: Israel and Babylonia. The Jewish theologians in both the Reform and Conservative camps expressed many uncertainties about Israel.

By the mid-1960s this, too, had changed. The theological fad had passed, the religious revival was over. Blacks and student radicals and the "beautiful people" replaced clergymen as the favorite interviewees on radio and TV shows. Poverty was a more favored newspaper topic than theology, and theology could no longer carry the burden of expressing one's Jewish identity. Furthermore, the theologians themselves turned a corner and placed Israel in the center of Jewish theological concerns.

Synagogue Activity

For all practical purposes, a religious definition of Judaism means synagogue affiliation. Regardless of what expression the American Jew found for his Jewish identity, assuming that it fell within some conception of religion, it was also in a context of or harmonious with synagogue affiliation. It was from his rabbi that the American Jew was warned of the dangers of anti-Semitism, reminded of the link between social justice and the prophets, informed about the needs of fellow Jews everywhere, and lectured to about Jewish theology. It was within the synagogue, though not only there, that meetings to combat anti-Semitism were held, social action committees were formed, fund raising for world Jewry or lecture series about world Jewry were held, and the latest books on theology were discussed, reviewed, and even sold.

Thus the focuses of Jewish expression which we have heretofore enumerated were all subsumed in a Jewish religious self-definition and synagogue activity. But there were some Jews whose expression of Jewish identity became the synagogue itself. For many Jews in the 1950s and early 1960s the preeminent Jewish activity, the form in which one expressed one's religious commitment, was activity on behalf of the synagogue —most especially fund-raising activity, but also in membership drives.

Countless hours were spent by tens if not hundreds of thousands of Jews in the planning and execution of dinners, bazaars, journals, theater benefits, and so on, for the purpose (at least ostensibly) of raising money to pay off the synagogue mortgage. During the 1950s American Jews engaged in fantastic efforts in synagogue-building. This activity, in turn, yielded enormous financial fruits. Not only were synagogues built, but by the mid-1960s many of them had either been paid for or were so financially secure that there was no question or concern about their financial future. What then was left for the layman to do?

Israel

There have always been Jews to whom Zionism or support for Israel was a primary expression of their Jewish identity. Israel's importance for them and its increasing significance for other Jews is discussed in greater detail in the next section. We only pause here to note that unlike such expressions of Jewish identity as the fight against anti-Semitism, the pursuit of social justice, the sense of peoplehood, Jewish theology, and synagogue activity, support for Israel retained its resonance into the late 1960s. For many Jews it was the only cause that was left. In addition to the other factors mentioned, Israel increased in importance simply because alternative expressions of Jewish identity had declined in importance by the mid-1960s.

Let us turn now to some of the positive factors that contributed to the rising importance of Israel in American Jewish life.

INCREASED IMPORTANCE OF ISRAEL

Israel has a special appeal for the nonreligious Jew, for the Jew who finds no outlet for his Jewish identification in a religious context. To him, Israel may be the carrier of a secular Jewish culture which has virtually disappeared in the United States. Israel's role as the representative of secular Judaism helps account for the fact that the Jewish Community Center movement, which was indifferent to Zionism prior to 1948, now makes it an important component of its programing. (What else is Jewish but not religious?) Israel's function as the model of secular Judaism also helps explain its popularity among some segments of radical Jewish youth, who are alienated from the synagogue and religion but still feel Jewish attachments. Indeed, pro-Israeli activity provides a marvelous opportunity for the radical youth to act out a rebellion against his family and against the Jewish establishment, while still remaining within the boundaries of community consensus.

Our concern, however, is with the bulk of American Jewry who in one way or another continue to view their Jewish identity as religious. What factors, other than the elimination of other expressions of Jewish identity discussed in the last section, account for Israel's increasing importance?

The Role of Religion

The Jewish religion itself stresses the importance of Israel. The Lakeville study referred to earlier found that the greater the involvement in synagogue life, the more frequent the attendance at religious services, and the more intensive the level of religious observance at home, the greater the level of support for Israel.[5] The authors point out that:

In sum, pro-Israel sentiment is sustained by some form of religious commitment. And commitment to Israel does not generally function as a substitute for Jewish observance, devotionalism, or involvement in synagogue affairs. Rather, for the Lakeville Jew pro-Israel sentiment goes hand in hand with religious commitment.[6]

Jewish prayers repeatedly recall the hope for a Jewish return to Zion and the rebuilding of the Temple (the latter hope, after all, touches the emotions of very few American Jews); the religious establishment, especially the various rabbinical and synagogue organizations, has been unanimous in their pronouncements and declarations in support of Israel; and, especially at the local congregational level, Israel has turned into a focal point of Jewish identity. The rabbis' sermons which stress Israel, the gift objects from Israel, the trips to Israel under synagogue auspices, the prominent place of Israel in men's club and sisterhood programing, and the increasing number of Israelis who staff the synagogue's school programs all attest to this.

Nothing illustrates Israel's role in the religious life of American Jewry better than the sale of Israel Bonds on Yom Kippur. This holiest day of the Jewish calendar stresses the personal relationship of man to God and the idea of repentance. The prayers, devoted to spiritual self-assessment and pleas for forgiveness, are interrupted in hundreds of synagogues in the United States by an appeal to the congregants to buy Israel Bonds. The point here is not whether such conduct is right or wrong, just or unjust, necessary or unnecessary. Let us grant that it may be the most effective way to raise money. It is nevertheless vulgar and ludicrous. But American Jews apparently don't consider it either vulgar or ludicrous, and this says a great deal about their concept of "religious" behavior and the place of Israel in their "religious" outlook.

The foregoing suggests that American Jews continue to define Judaism as a religion but that Israel increasingly defines the content of that religion. Concomitantly, support for Israel becomes not merely support for a state thousands of miles away or for its inhabitants; rather, support for Israel is the symbol of one's Jewish identity, like staying home from work on Yom

Kippur. It has nothing to do with Zionism, with a national Jewish self-definition, or even with knowing very much about Israel itself or modern Jewish-Israeli culture. It is perfectly compatible with being a good American.[7] Of course, there are other reasons as well for the important place of Israel in American Jewish life.

Stakes

The stakes involved in Israel's success are obvious. Over two million Jewish lives are involved. Furthermore, unlike Soviet Jewry, far more American Jews have relatives in Israel whom they have met, whom they continue to hear from, and with whom they may even correspond regularly.

Secular Outlet

Support for Israel, politically and financially, represents an outlet and expression of Jewish activity which is religiously legitimate, but which is entirely secular in content. In a sense it gives one something Jewish and something important to do which—unlike pure religious behavior—demands no knowledge and no strange ritualized behavior. Indeed, it permits the Jew to do what he excels at—fund raising and organization.

Mass Media

The mass media bring Israel to the constant attention of the American Jew. The agenda of American Jewish life is by and large dictated by the concerns of the non-Jewish media. Religion, as we indicated, is no longer the topic of as many articles, news stories, books, nor are religious personalities the subject of as many TV interviews, as they were in the last two decades. But Israel has achieved much greater prominence, thereby reinforcing the efforts of Jewish leaders to bring its problems to the attention of American Jews. Hardly a day goes by that news from or about Israel is not featured in a newspaper or mentioned on TV. Such stories constantly remind the Jew of his attachment to Israel, and they also stress that Israel is "the Jewish thing."

The Reward System

One striking phenomenon about Israel's role in Jewish life is that it has enlisted support from the least likely sources: virtually assimilated Jews, including the very wealthy who heretofore confined their major philanthropy to non-Jewish institutions (universities, museums, and the like) or to loosely affiliated Jewish institutions—such as hospitals whose only tie to Judaism is their name (suggesting their origin as Jewish institutions) or the fact that the rich laymen on the board of directors are Jewish. Yet many of these same Jews have contributed substantial sums of money to Israel and number themselves among its staunchest friends.

The reason for this may rest in part on the secular possibilities already mentioned which activity in behalf of Israel affords. One can work for Israel without doing anything "Jewish." Zionism was always able to attract a certain assimilated element—in part because, despite the Jewish goal of Zionism, there was nothing Jewish about the manner in which the objectives were to be achieved. On the contrary, organization at the international level, diplomacy, and national politics had, after two thousand years of Jewish statelessness, a distinctly gentile flavor.

But there are more compelling reasons for Israel's popularity among that element of Jews who were never attracted to Zionism before the creation of the State of Israel; and these reasons also help to account for its importance among other Jews. There is no other institution in the world which is the recipient of private philanthropy and which can confer the status or rewards upon its contributors equal to that of the State of Israel. Israel may be a tiny, poor, and beleaguered country which is dependent upon the goodwill and charity of its friends abroad (as it was once portrayed in the fund-raising activity in its behalf), but it is a *state*—a member of the United Nations with duly authorized representatives in all major cities of the United States, having an army which is universally feared or admired and a prime minister and minister of defense who are recognized all over the world. What can Harvard University or the Metropolitan Museum, not to mention Mt. Sinai Hospital or Brandeis University, do to compete with a luncheon given by Golda Meir, a trip to the Suez Canal accompanied by an Israeli general, dinner with the ambassador, or a private word from Moshe Dayan? Israel provides a graded reward system which at the lower echelons includes plaques, certificates, and jewelry, and at the pinnacle reaches far beyond that which any private institution can provide.

The *Heim*

While Israel's image as an autonomous state sitting with the mighty nations of the world increases its importance to one set of American Jews, Israel as a replacement of the East European *heim* has added to its importance among a second group. *Heim* is a Yiddish word. Its literal meaning is "home," with all the connotations of warmth and security and with all the nostalgia that surround the concept home. Its meaning may be captured more accurately if it is translated as "the old home."

To many American Jews, the *heim* prior to World War II was Eastern Europe. To some American Jews, especially those of the younger generation, the concept *heim* had no meaning. But there were others, including some born in the United States, to whom the *heim* was a meaningful referent. Indeed, sometimes it appeared that the farther removed from Eastern Europe the Jew was, the more lovingly he evoked its memories. What was most remarkable about the *heim*, what makes it really "the old home," is that for all the love, warmth, and security that it recalled, American Jews did not want to live there. It was really the parents' home. It was the home which the young adult leaves, to which he returns at most for a visit, but which he senses that he has in some way outgrown.

Six million Jews were murdered by the Nazis; Jewish life in Eastern Europe was virtually obliterated; and as a result the *heim* disappeared. It took a number of years before the disappearance of the *heim* sank into the consciousness of American Jews. Nor did this consequence of the holocaust affect all Jews equally. Many of those who were emotionally affected found a substitute *heim* in Israel. Now, the characteristic of the *heim*, as we noted, is that one doesn't live there. It is the parents' home, or in the case of Israel the surrogate parents' and surrogate grandparents' home. One visits it on occasion, one sends money (without ever having the bad taste to inquire how that money is spent), and one wants very much to feel that life goes on there as it always has (which is why the type of Jew to whom Israel is *heim* expects and wants all Israelis to be religious, regardless of how uninterested he himself may be in religion). This type of Jew is more likely to be indignant at any public criticism of Israel and takes a particular delight in how old-fashioned or quaint he imagines Israel to be. This is the Jew who is quite certain he would be completely at home in Israel, though he knows very little about the country and makes no special effort to learn anything.

The sense of Israel as the *heim* was invoked in a remarkable document: the warning issued by Rabbi Meir Kahane, leader of the Jewish Defense League, to the Jews of America in 1970.[8] Kahane warns Jews of the physical destruction that awaits them in America from anti-Semites of all sorts, and he urges them to move to Israel. But he never once mentions the word Israel. Instead, he constantly returns to the theme with which his statement begins: "The time has come to return home." Kahane's primary audience—the poor, mostly elderly Jews of the slums, who are fearful of violence to themselves and their property—feel increasingly ill at ease in the climate and culture of the big cities. Though Jews were traditionally more urban in orientation than any other group, this generation feels uncomfortable (not *at home*) with the new urban culture. It is not Israel as the mighty nation that evokes emotional stirrings among them, but rather Israel as a *heim*.

PROSPECTS

As long as the American Jew values both survival and integration, Israel can never represent more than a symbol of Jewish identification. His support for Israel must always be balanced against the limitations of acceptance by American society. Paradoxically, one sign of assimilation's inroads among American Jews is the fact they have such self-confidence and feel so at home in the environment that their support for Israel is not instinctively balanced by the specter of dual loyalty or disloyalty to America. Obviously, all this is helped by the fact that Israeli and American policies are so harmonious today. Thus, at least for the present, American Jews are likely to continue to identify with Israel, and Gentiles will have to do more than gently prod them before they realize that their enthusiasm for Israel may have exceeded the society's boundaries of acceptable behavior. Only twenty years ago American Jews were far more sensitive to questions of dual loyalty. They were far more likely to raise the issue themselves, before *Time* magazine or Christian clergymen alluded to it. To this we must add, however, that Black Power and similar slogans have legitimized ethnic group self-interest and autonomous political activity in an unprecedented way.

Conditions change. Negroes may once again revive the slogans of integration and moderation; American foreign policy may become less compatible with that of Israel; assimilation may continue to erode survival values; or a new religious revival might occur. Any of these changes might decrease the signal role which Israel now plays in the consciousness and identification of the American Jews.

PART TWO:

Integration and Survival
in Its American
Resolution

FOREWORD TO PART TWO

Part one dealt with the formation of the American Jewish community and the emergence of its religious identity as a response to the twin values of integration and survival. In the last chapter we saw how even American Jewish concern for Israel reflects these twin values and reinforces the religious self-definition, by providing content and symbols to the American Jewish religion, which stood in danger of erosion.

Part two is concerned with the resolution of the integration-survival values in various settings. We have suggested that these values are in tension with one another and that Jews and subgroups of Jews must resolve these tensions. In the next two chapters, two subgroups are presented—rabbinical students and Jewish youth—in order to explore how different kinds of groups reflect and reconcile these tensions. In chapter 7 we note that integration and survival lead Jews not only to alter their behavior but also to seek to alter their political environment— through political liberalism. The final chapter of part two focuses on radical Jewish students, whose behavior disturbed the general and Jewish community in the late 1960s. Their behavior may be viewed as an effort to reshape their environment, but it is also the behavior characteristic of a very special group of highly assimilated Jews for whom the values, and hence the tensions, of survival and integration no longer play a critical role. The chapter concludes on the paradoxical note that escape from these tensions is not always possible even when the twin values are not internalized by the actors themselves.

5

RABBINICAL STUDENTS

The institutions of the Jewish community and Jews themselves are sometimes viewed, particularly by other Jews, as
falling along a continuum between self-segregation and assimilation. Self-segregation represents the desire for group survival;
assimilation, the desire for acceptance by American culture.
Using this crude model, observers have sought to locate and
compare Jews and Jewish institutions as they fall closer to one
or the other end of the continuum. But the model is much too
simplistic. In addition to the simple fact that we lack a variable
to define the continuum, the model overlooks at least two crucial aspects of American Jewish life.

Institutions which are by their structure uniquely Jewish may
serve the latent function of assimilating the Jew to aspects of
American culture. This is precisely the role which the Yiddish
press fulfilled for immigrant Jews at the turn of the century. It
was through the medium of the Yiddish press that immigrants
learned middle-class mores and etiquette, American values of
child rearing, connubial relations, romantic love, women's new
emancipated role, and political participation.[1] Jewish fraternal
organizations provide an opportunity for Jews to meet socially,
and through their adult-education programs they reinforce values of group survival. But social activities such as a weekend in

Las Vegas, a fishing trip, or a synagogue dinner dance or cocktail party may introduce the member to aspects of non-Jewish leisure activity which may suggest a whole new set of values and attitudes, a whole new life-style. The program of the Torah Lodge of B'nai B'rith in Baltimore, which featured Miss Libbie Jones discussing "The Psychology of Stripteasing," probably threatened more than strengthened Jewish group survival.

On the other hand, increased ease in America may strengthen Jewish group values. We have already had occasion to note that the surge of support for Israel is partially explained by the fact that the American Jew feels so at home in America that he is no longer troubled by fears of dual-loyalty charges. Left-wing intellectuals and radicals of the 1930s who denied their Jewish heritage and went so far as to affirm the insignificance of Hitler's anti-Semitism were led back to a sense of Jewishness as they were led back to an affirmation of the positive aspects of American life.[2] One writer noted that the more Americanized the Jewish workers became, "the more enthusiastically they support[ed] the fund for Palestine and the Jewish State."[3]

Thus the impact of organizational membership and activity or acculturation on Jewish survival is complex. Institutions are not easily located along a continuum from self-segregation to assimilation if the result of membership in the nominally more survivalist or self-segregated group leads to rapid assimilation; whereas affirmation of American values may be coincident with greater Jewish commitment.

A similar problem exists when we attempt to locate individual Jews along a continuum. Virtually every Jew is affected by both polarities. It is often difficult to determine whether Jewish activities in a Jewish organization fulfill Jewish survival needs or whether they are simply an instrument whereby the Jew can hope to engage in contact with the broader society by virtue of his status as a Jewish leader. If, indeed, almost all Jews seek both survival and integration, then participation in Jewish life may not be incompatible with participation in non-Jewish life as well. On the contrary, the more time or money one contributes to Jewish causes, the greater the compulsion may be toward participation in non-Jewish affairs.

This ambiguity is found not only among the masses of American Jews; it is even present among their leaders. Indeed, it finds clear expression among those whose Jewish identity is most clearly established: the American rabbi. The rabbi is, in many respects, the quintessential Jew. He cannot hide his Jewish identity—it is the basic fact of his life and determines his economic and professional as well as his social and cultural status. The rabbinical role is by definition a Jewishly activist role. But, we suggest, it also raises the problem of one's American identity more critically than does any other occupational role. It is in his rabbinical school, as the rabbi undergoes his professional training, that the rabbi's self-definition and self-identity as both a Jew and an American receive their basic formulation.

The data upon which this chapter draws are based on a 1967 survey of rabbinical students at the leading Orthodox and Conservative rabbinical seminaries: Yeshiva University (YU) and the Jewish Theological Seminary of America (JTS).[4] For purposes of this chapter, rabbinical students who anticipate careers as congregational rabbis are compared with those who are not studying for any career purpose, or who intend utilizing their studies for careers such as educators. No data are reported for Reform rabbinical students, since virtually all of them reported intentions of becoming congregational rabbis. The Orthodox and Conservative rabbinical students who intend to become congregational rabbis are hereafter referred to as future rabbis; Orthodox and Conservative rabbinical students who do not intend to become congregational rabbis are hereafter referred to as nonrabbis—something of a misnomer, since all will be entitled to bear the title rabbi.

Our hypothesis is that as rabbinical students advance from their first to last year, future rabbis, through a process of anticipatory socialization, will reflect more accurately than non-rabbis the ambiguities and tensions that are characteristic of the American Jewish community. The nonrabbi who devotes three to six years of his life to intensive study of Jewish sources, without always intending to utilize this knowledge for career purposes, is the iconoclast who is more likely to deviate from the standards and the characteristic attitudes of the American Jewish community than is the future rabbi.

This is especially true because the rabbi's role in the community is one of representation rather than one of leadership. Any such generalization understates the role of a number of rabbis who have been innovative. But looking at the American Jewish community in its entirety, it seems fair to observe that initiative in communal matters has come from such secular Jewish organizations as the American Jewish Congress, the American Jewish Committee, the Student Struggle for Soviet Jewry, and the Jewish Defense League, rather than from religious organizations. Since the primary institutional mode of identification between the Jew and the Jewish community is the synagogue, the rabbi is an important channel through which secular Jewish agencies may reach the American Jew.

But the rabbi is not the leader.[5] The communal issues upon which the rabbi may take a stand are limited by the prevailing ideologies which owe their impetus to forces outside the synagogue. The rabbi must be for Jewish unity, he must favor better relations with non-Jews, he must be sympathetic to and support the State of Israel; in most cases he must favor separation of church and state, and he must not have a "ghetto mentality" and favor withdrawal of the Jewish community from the mainstream of American life. In short, he must embody the values of both Jewish identity and participation in American life. In matters of ritual observance and belief most rabbis are certainly little more than exemplary figures. With some exceptions the rabbi cannot meaningfully challenge his congregants to increased observance, though he may occasionally exhort them in this regard. Rather, the Orthodox and Conservative rabbis are expected to act out ritual observance in their public and private life and serve as a model for the young, perhaps thereby also expiating the sins of the adults. It should not surprise us, therefore, if future rabbis embody the values of the American Jewish community more closely than do the nonrabbis.

All first- and last-year rabbinical students were asked whether they spent their leisure time in all or mostly all Jewish activity, in all or mostly all non-Jewish activity, or whether it was fairly evenly divided between Jewish and non-Jewish activity. Our hypothesis is that in view of the distinctively Jewish image of the congregational rabbi, he would, as it were, compensate for this by participating more vigorously in non-Jewish activity.

TABLE 5.1   Leisure-Time Activity

Activity	Future rabbis			Nonrabbis		
	first yr. %	last yr. %	% difference	first yr. %	last yr. %	% difference
All or mostly Jewish	35	17	−18	35	53	+18
Evenly divided	43	57	+14	52	38	−14
All or mostly non-Jewish	22	25	+3	14	8	−6
	N=23*	N=24		N=29	N=13	

*N=number of persons surveyed

The data indicate that between their first and last year the proportion of nonrabbis who spend most of their leisure time in Jewish activity increases, whereas the proportion of future rabbis who do so decreases. This finding is further reinforced by students' responses to the question of whether they had attended an opera, concert, or play in the past six months. Among nonrabbis there was a decrease of 20 percent between first- and last-year students, but future rabbis did not decrease their attendance.

Students were also asked whether they had participated in

programs of social action during the past year and, if so, in what type. At YU social action is a very minor feature of student life. Less than one-third of last-year students had participated in any program. However, this is not the case at JTS. The Conservative rabbinate, the student culture, and a number of faculty members all support such activity as an outgrowth of personal religious concern. The future rabbis at JTS increased their participation in exclusively non-Jewish social-action programs between their first and last year (from 8 percent to 23 percent), whereas among nonrabbis participation in such activity declined slightly, from 25 percent to 17 percent. Of course, we are dealing with a very small sample where differences of only one student are reflected in large percentage changes, but the findings do support the hypothesis and reinforce the impressions gained from personal interviews with students and alumni.

It may be argued that what has occurred is not a change in student attitude between the first and last year but rather a redistribution in the type of student who does or does not intend to become a congregational rabbi. This is possible, but it in no way negates the thrust of our findings. What it means is that the student who has more exclusive Jewish concerns now finds the rabbinate increasingly less attractive as he gets closer to ordination, and the student with diverse interests finds the position of "Jewish professional" increasingly attractive. Interviews with students and faculty, however, suggest that the data are best explained by changes in the attitudes of the students themselves, rather than by changes in career choices.

The twin values of integration and survival have, as we suggested, implications for the definition of American Judaism. It has led to an essentially religious definition, with the problems attendant on the fact that Judaism is not, after all, a religion in the same sense that Christianity is a religion. As we have pointed out, many of the characteristics of American Jews—the importance they attach to family and social ties within a Jewish framework, their emphasis on associational bonds—are characteristic of an ethnic rather than a religious group. The fact that American Jews created a religious structure within which they carried out essentially ethnic activity helps explain the emergence of the rabbi as the nominal Jewish leader (who else but a clergyman can lead a religious group?), his significance as an exemplary figure, and his potential irrelevance to what many Jews consider the basic business of the Jewish community: helping other Jews, retaining a sense of Jewish identity, and providing a Jewish context for one's interpersonal relationships.

We may assume that the rabbinical student's initial attraction to his seminary studies derives from religious motivations. We might also assume, other things being equal, that a rabbinical school would reinforce religious rather than ethnic conceptions of and orientations to Judaism. Yet as the future rabbi becomes socialized to his profession, to the interests and needs of the American Jewish community, to maximizing his role in the community, we might expect him to balance his religious orientation with an ethnic one more than nonrabbis would.

Students were asked to indicate which problems facing American Jewry they felt to be of the highest priority. In table 5.2 we have grouped these problems into religious, ethnic-communal, and other problems.[6]

TABLE 5.2   Most Important Problems Facing American Jews

Problem	Future rabbis			Nonrabbis		
	first yr. %	last yr. %	% difference	first yr. %	last yr. %	% difference
Religious	26	12	−14	35	23	−12
Ethnic-communal	18	41	+23	28	30	+2
Other	56	46	−10	38	46	+8
	N=23*	N=24		N=29	N=13	

*N=number of persons surveyed

In contrast to nonrabbis, future rabbis show a great increase in the proportion who believe, by their last year, that ethnic-communal problems are of the highest priority. The differential changes between rabbis and nonrabbis with respect to religious problems do not appear to be great. However, problems of Jewish education, which were placed in the category "other," might have more properly been labeled "religious problems." In that case we would have found a sharp drop in the proportion of future rabbis who checked religious problems as those having highest priority and virtually no change among nonrabbis between their first and last year.

Students were also asked, regardless of whether they did or did not intend to become congregational rabbis, to check which aspects of the rabbinate they considered most attractive. In table 5.3 their responses are divided into religious and other aspects of the rabbinate.[7] Our hypothesis would be that nonrabbis would be more likely than future rabbis to find religious aspects of the rabbinate attractive between their first and last years.

TABLE 5.3 Most Attractive Aspects of the Rabbinate

	Future rabbis			Nonrabbis		
Aspect	first yr. %	last yr. %	% difference	first yr. %	last yr. %	% difference
Religious	52	66	+14	52	86	+34
Other	48	33	−15	48	15	−33
	N=23*	N=24		N=29	N=13	

*N=number of persons surveyed

Our hypothesis is confirmed in table 5.3, although, somewhat surprisingly, the proportion of both future rabbis and nonrabbis who find religious aspects of the rabbinate to be the most attractive ones increases between the first and last years.

In contrast to the nonrabbi, we find the future rabbi on the verge of entering his chosen career to have become more sensitized to the realities of American Jewish life, or at least more attuned to them. The future rabbi's own activity and attitudes toward Jewish life are now in closer harmony with those of other Jews than was the case when he first entered rabbinical school. The American Jewish community, one may say, begins to shape its future leaders before these leaders have had their first chance to shape the community.

6

JEWISH YOUTH*

The Jewish baby does not emerge from its mother's womb torn between values of integration and survival. Indeed, as we shall see, Jewish youths are quite naive about the existence of the tension. While their parents seek to suppress it, the children simply fail to recognize it. But this does not mean that Jewish youths gravitate to one or the other end of a survival-integration continuum.

As is true of the adult community, one can find Jewish youth ranging all along the continuum. There are those whose Jewish identification is very high and those for whom it is very low. Among the youth, as among adults, one of the best measures for distinguishing Jewish identification is the degree of religious traditionalism. For example, there is a significant relationship between religious traditionalism and a preference for Jewish companionship, a tendency to emphasize Jewish group solidarity, or a resistance to adopting non-Jewish practices and opin-

---

*Efforts to understand American Jews are handicapped by the absence of data. This is particularly true with respect to the study of American Jewish youth; information is at best fragmentary and sporadic. Thus one must rely primarily on anecdotal and impressionistic observations, supplemented by the few reliable studies that exist. Conclusions in this chapter should really be treated as suggestions.

ions.[1] The association between Jewish identification and traditionalism remains even after holding constant the factor of home environment. Bernard Rosen found that among adolescents from nonobservant homes, "high identifiers were five times as likely to be traditionalistic in beliefs, three times as likely to be traditionalistic in attitudes toward practice, and nine times as likely to be traditionalistic in actual behavior than were low identifiers from a similar home environment."[2]

Were we to focus exclusively on those whose Jewish identification was very high or very low, however, we would not only exclude the vast majority of Jewish youth, but we would also overlook the most striking characteristic of Jewish youth: their seemingly paradoxical attitudes and behavior. We know, for example, that the Jewish people cannot survive with a high rate of intermarriage. Yet in a sample study of Jewish youth in New Orleans, 57 percent of the girls and 77 percent of the boys agreed that a person should marry someone he loves without regard to religion.[3] Among twelfth graders, 90 percent of the boys agreed with the statement.[4] Furthermore, 93 percent of the twelfth graders in the sample had interdated.[5] If ever a Jewish group appeared destined for oblivion, New Orleans youth would seem to qualify. Nevertheless, 92 percent of the same sample reported that they expected to conduct a seder (a ceremonial family meal eaten the first and second nights of the Passover holiday) in their future homes, and more than two-thirds said they would own Jewish books, pictures, and art objects.[6] Every study of Jewish youths finds that they feel a sense of attachment to the Jewish community.

How are we to explain these contradictory findings? Our answer is that Jewish youths accept the manifest (public) values of their parents but lack the sophisticated rationalizations to reconcile the contradictions between the manifest and latent values of the Jewish community. They act out their parents' public values, often to the chagrin and disappointment of their parents, who don't really always value what they say they value, or want what they say they want. We shall try to examine this process as carefully as the available data will enable us to.

THE RELIGIOUS SELF-DEFINITION AND YOUTH'S ACQUIESCENCE

Jewish youths of high school age accept the public religious values of their parents. Indeed, they are inclined to be more traditionalistic than their parents. We noted, for example, that 92 percent of the New Orleans teen-agers stated their intention to conduct a seder in their future homes. An earlier study had reported that only 67 percent of the parents of students in New Orleans religious schools actually held seders.[7] In their study of Riverton, a middle-sized northeastern industrial town, Sklare and Vosk found that 83 percent of the youth approved of the Jewish customs observed in their parents' homes. Even those who reported negative feelings were not rebellious. In the 13–15 age group, only 5 percent intended to observe less than their parents and over 10 percent planned to observe more.[8] The authors of the Riverton study asked their sample of parents and children the following question: "If you were being reborn, would you prefer to remain a Jew or be born into another religion?" Eighty-two percent of the parents—but 88 percent of their teen-age children—said they would prefer to be reborn a Jew.[9]

Young people accept the American definition of Judaism as a religion. If they are to be Jewish, therefore, they must act out their Jewishness religiously. Sklare and Vosk found that 80 percent of the parents and 97 percent of the adolescents defined a Jew by his allegiance to the Jewish religion.[10] But differences between generations on the meaning of Judaism were even more striking than agreement on what the label *religion* implies. In response to the question of why Jews should continue as a group, the authors comment as follows:

Parents showed their awareness of age-old hostility between Jew and non-Jew, while children emphasized the virtues of Judaism and Jewishness. The parents were viewing the Jews partly as a culture which has a right to exist; the children were thinking in terms of a religion which forms part of the American harmony. The parents responded in the framework of a wide gulf separating Jews from the Gentile world; the children did not see this gulf.[11]

In one study an adolescent defined being Jewish in this way: "A person is a Jew because you believe in Jewish ideals; it's the way you observe the things you do, like going to the synagogue. You're a good religious person."[12] Substitute the word Christian for Jew and church for synagogue and one might have the definition the average Christian would give for his religion. For the descendants of East European Jews, however, this is certainly a novel definition. It is not radically different from what youths observe their parents paying lip service to. The difference is that fewer of the parents are likely to believe the public definition.

Parents may talk about Judaism as a religion, but Judaism is symbolized and reinforced by familistic memories and nostalgia, unique consumption patterns, linguistic expressions, and social relations. Since this is hardly a legitimate ground for group recognition in America, Judaism is defined, at least publicly, as a religion. This redefinition or reinterpretation has resulted in real changes in the Jews' own self-perception. The process reaches its logical extension in the children. They are quite acquiescent toward the *religion* of their parents. In fact, there is an association between what parents expect Jewishly from their children and how the children in turn think and behave.[13]

Youths' perception of their parents' expectations reinforces the religious rather than the ethnic definition of Judaism. In the New Orleans study, 75 percent of the respondents thought their fathers would not mind if they spent most of their time with non-Jewish friends of the same sex.[14]

INTEGRATION AND SURVIVAL

In view of the findings that Jewish youths are positively identified with the Jewish community and oppose assimilation, how can we explain the high rate of interdating or the finding that more teen-agers expect to exchange Christmas presents in their future families than to keep a kosher home?[15] Youth is again expressing the conflicting values of its parents. Let us take New Orleans as an example. Seventy-two percent of a sample of Jewish adults agreed that "Jewish people have a strong obligation to continue the Jewish way of life regardless of what other groups in the community might think."[16] Presumably this is an affirmation of survival values. But the expression of this value is not viewed by the parents as conflicting with their desire for integration in the community. In fact, an even higher proportion of adults—over 90 percent—agreed with the statement that "insofar as possible, Jewish people should try to fit in with the community rather than trying to keep themselves separate in any way."[17]

We can now suggest how youth interprets the conflicting values of its parents. Judaism is defined religiously. Hence the maxim that the "Jewish people have a strong obligation to continue the Jewish way of life" means that the good Jew should have a seder, attend synagogue, light Hanukah candles, but above all else "accept being a good Jew and not try to hide it."[18] The demand, however, that the "Jewish people should try to fit in with the community rather than trying to keep themselves separate" has implications for the ethnic or communal basis of Judaism. It means that one can interdate and exchange Christmas presents, because to do otherwise is to keep oneself separate. It also means, at the attitudinal level, that a majority of youths reject the traditional notion of Jews as a "chosen people."[19] It is true that young people misunderstand the concept theologically and misinterpret it as a denial of the equality of man. But in all likelihood this is how the folk religion always

interpreted "chosen people." Youth denies the concept because it certainly is an obstacle to social and ideological integration.

EXPLAINING PARENTAL INFLUENCE

Jewish parents, it appears, do influence their adolescent children Jewishly, and the religious behavior of Jewish youths can
be explained as the refraction, if not the reflection, of their
parents' attitudes and behavior. Most young people not only
look to their parents in the exercise of religious rites but also
estimate their own religiosity and judge themselves Jewishly by
the religious attitudes and behavior of their family.[20] Indeed,
neither their friends nor their rabbi (the institutionalized
bearer of the religious tradition) nor even the tradition itself
serves as a religious model as often as the family does.

This finding should give us pause. How does one explain the
strong influence of parents over the religious behavior of Jewish
teen-agers? Rosen has written that adolescence is a period of
conflict between physiological and social maturity. It is a period
of tension for youths, who are often unsure of their own role and
adult expectations. In this period, adolescents turn to their
peers "for companionship, recognition and support."[21] Now
Rosen did find that when parents and peer groups differed over
such matters as using kosher meat, more teen-agers agreed with
their peer group than with their parents. In the fifty cases he
studied, such instances only occurred 28 percent of the time.
Fourteen percent of the time the reverse occurred, that is,
youths agreed with parents and disagreed with peers. Half the
time there was agreement between parents and peers over
religious norms that the young people followed.[22] Rosen's
findings suggest strong parental influence, which is especially
surprising in view of the apparent expansion in the influence of
youth culture.

Self-conscious stratification of American society is probably increasing most rapidly in two dimensions: occupation and age. Increasingly, one's identity is expressed through occupational and age groups rather than, for example, ethnic or religious or income groups. Age groupings are particularly salient at the teen-age and elderly end of the spectrum. Youth is increasingly recognized as a special market for purposes of consumption; it has its own art forms, magazines, books, and organizations. It has even gained legitimacy as a semiautonomous group in the society, with the right to demand federal allocations or jobs— though its spokesmen are adults. Adolescence is no longer perceived simply as a transitional period or a preparation for adulthood. Though the society continues its efforts to socialize the teen-ager for adult roles, the thrust of high school education, the mass media, and the economic system has been toward the recognition of youth as a distinct group, not a time span. The consequences are that youth is dealt with in terms of its problems and its perceptions of its own needs. This has enhanced the importance of youth as an identity expression. It has led, for example, to the phenomenon of youth heroes who are not, as they once were, adults, but rather are themselves youths. Teenagers today, perhaps for the first time, find their culture heroes in other teen-agers or in Hollywood's pretend teen-agers, rather than in the adult community. The characteristic which the teen-age heroes share is their rejection of adult society, adult values, and adult authority.

Under these circumstances we might anticipate the evolution of specialized religious structures for youth, or a change in religious structures that cater to youth, from an emphasis on preparing teen-agers for adulthood to an emphasis on coping with the special religious problems or the particular religious condition of youth. To the extent that they have developed, such structures further destroy the adolescent's perception of his parents as a religious model.

Nevertheless, despite all the influences which would tend to magnify peer group rather than parental influence among young people, Jewish youths still look to their family as a religious model. One study found that more than two out of three young people preferred their parents to any other companions for attendance at religious services.[23] How do we explain this influence?

One explanation is that Jewish youths are different from non-Jewish American youths. This is not the way observers see them, however, or, for that matter, the way Jewish youth see themselves. David Boroff, in his study of Jewish teen-agers, found that they participated fully in American teen-age culture without any sense of uniqueness or special destiny. He quoted as typical a girl who defined herself as a "teen-ager of Jewish parents."[24]

An alternative explanation for the receptivity of Jewish adolescents to parental influence in Jewish matters is the essential triviality of Judaism and Jewish observance in the lives of most teen-agers. Although Jewish youths agree that one must be a Jew and be proud of it, this affirmation is of no consequence in the larger order of the adolescent's life. The most apt analogy to Judaism and Jewish observance for most Jewish youth may well be the act of brushing one's teeth in the morning. One has to do it, one might even enjoy it, and if one doesn't do it others may find out. Certainly the dentist will eventually catch up with one. It is hardly an activity which engages one's mind, energy, or attention the rest of the day, however. To carry the analogy further, the message of the synagogue is like the TV commercial that tells one to brush after every meal. One knows the commercial is right, but its net effect is, at most, to make one feel a little guilty.

Religion is symbolized by parent and home. At its most positive, it represents something warm and comfortable to teenagers. Asked to describe how they felt at synagogue services, the most frequently chosen word was "peaceful."[25] Judaism does not engage the effort or energy of young people, nor is it a source of excitement or adventure. It does not call them to the radically different or to the radically *other*. It is not perceived as making demands of a more than formalistic nature. It simply does not merit rebellion.

THE COLLEGE EXPERIENCE

The religious acquiesence of Jewish youths undergoes a change in college. We noted that they had engaged in religious activity and had formed peer-group associations, primarily among other Jews, in high school. But Jewish associations and activity are not inconsistent with a non-Jewish life-style and behavior patterns. Only the structure or shell of these patterns was Jewish, and this is easily broken in college. Away from home, the contradictions or tensions which define the Jewish home may appear more obvious and unattractive. There is an absence on the college campus of positive Jewish figures who command deference and respect. Most significantly, as college students find new intellectual challenges, the excitement of new horizons, the sense of power associated with greater physical and social independence, and confrontation with new groups of people, the homes they left dwindle on their scale of values. Those activities associated with the home, in our case Judaism, lose the meaning they once might have had. Even the "pleasant" and "peaceful" synagogue is now recalled as an experience of childhood which one outgrows—a parochialism which must be submerged in the universalist order which is so demanding and at the same time so attractive. A national sample of American graduate students, for example, found that of those who reported themselves as being born Jewish, 33 percent now reported themselves as having no religion. Comparable figures for Protestants and Catholics were 25 percent and 12 percent respectively.[26] This is a serious problem for Judaism, however, not only because the Jewish percentage is higher, but also because a much higher proportion of Jews than non-Jews attend graduate school.

Among both graduate and undergraduate students of all religious backgrounds, the higher the quality of the school, the more likely the student is to give up his religious ties.[27] Even those who continued to identify themselves as Jewish are less religious than their Christian peers. The percentage of Jewish students who reported a low level or no level of religious involvment varied from 94 percent at high-quality graduate schools to 85 percent at low-quality schools. The range for Protestants, on the other hand, was 70 percent to 56 percent and for Catholics 37 percent to 11 percent.[28] To cite one other example, a survey of 208 students enrolled in three sociology courses at the University of Michigan found that 86 percent of the Catholics, 64 percent of the Protestants, but *none* of the 38 Jews attended religious services twice a month or more.[29]

Unquestionably, some of these college youths are resocialized into the Jewish community once they marry and have children. But the problem for Judaism on the college campus and the aftereffects of the college experience remain acute.

We have been dealing here in an impressionistic way with the behavior of the masses of Jewish youth and college students over the past few decades. We have ignored the radical Jewish youth, whom we discuss in chapter 8; but we have also ignored the fact that in the last few years there has been increased interest on the part of many Jewish students with Judaism and things Jewish. The causes of this phenomenon, however, must be better understood before it can give the Jewish community much cause for rejoicing. It is related, in my opinion, to the decline of the American university.

The college experience to many, perhaps most, Jewish youths has in the past been so total and so liberating, the marvel of it and the universalistic feeling that it evoked so encompassing, that it left no room for Judaism. Not all the Jewish students experienced the university in the same way. Not all the Jewish students who shared the same experience understood it in the same way. For some, the university was institutionalized knowledge, rationality. Rationality is, by definition, universal. Its style is one of detachment. But rationality as an ultimate value and detachment as a style stand in a certain tension with Judaism.

Others experienced the university, not as institutionalized knowledge, but as a moral community, as a totalistic community in which one wants to live. As such, it certainly cut across and made irrelevant distinctions between Jew and Catholic and Protestant.

For still others, the university experience represented a context for individual self-expression—for learning, perhaps for the first time, that since people are different, one is an individual —not just part of a family or a religious group but also a singular entity. It was a glorious experience of freedom, a sense of personal liberation, which until recently found its primary (though not exclusive) expression on the American college campus in the sloughing off of restraints on sexual conduct. This experience, as well, excluded Judaism, which was not only constrictive but carried overtones of family and community from which one sought liberation.

Today we are experiencing the decline of the university, or, more properly, a decline in the centrality of the university to one's life experience. Students in American universities no longer believe that the university is the institutionalization of "real" knowledge. It is not, after all, the "real thing" that is taught in the college classrooms. Students want their own courses and want to organize their own classes, because they want to get to the "real" kind of knowledge. On the other hand, the value of knowledge, and of rationality itself, has declined in students' eyes. So the university becomes more trivial.

Finally, the experience of liberation, the finding of personal identity, the break from the home and its expression through sexual activity and drug use, has been pushed back to the high school and the junior high school. The university, then, is no longer a context for personal liberation. The university has become, if anything, a place to choose alternatives—and Judaism now has become a "serious" alternative. Serious, in quotation marks, because it is not Judaism that has become an alternative on the college campus but rather the *promise* of Judaism. It is the *promise* of Judaism that is pitted against the reality of the university. In the students' experience the university is a failure, and they search for something else. In their search for alternatives, many students are even willing to consider the possibility that Judaism has something to offer. Judaism can do quite well in such a context, at least in a superficial way and in a relative sense to what it was doing ten or twenty years ago.

But this is a very cheap victory. In the promise of Judaism against the reality of the university—Judaism wins. Fifty years ago it was the reality of Judaism pitted against the promise of the university, and the university won. In the reality of Judaism against the reality of the university, it is probably the promise of something else that wins: the promise of Buddhism, the promise of magic, the promise of love, and so on. Judaism not only requires too much work and too much knowledge, but when properly understood its values are simply too idiosyncratic for the secular assumptions of the modern world.

We have, of course, overlooked the numerically small but sociologically important phenomenon of college groups such as Yavneh, which affirm traditional Judaism and find they can attract students from nonobservant homes. What one finds so interesting about the vitality of Orthodox Judaism on college campuses these past ten years is that many young people from nonobservant homes are first attracted by religious symbols which are ritually of least importance. Particularly noteworthy is the wearing of yarmulkes (skullcaps). Jewish religious law requires one to cover one's head when outdoors or when reciting a blessing. German Orthodox Jews, for example, did not cover their heads indoors. Nevertheless, the yarmulke has assumed enormous symbolic significance in the United States, because it is such an obvious and distinguishable symbol of the

Jewish identity which attracts an increasing, though small, number of college students.

In addition to the Orthodox, there are now to be found radical Jewishly committed youth from whose pens, for example, has evolved a student press of a magnitude heretofore unknown on college campuses.[30]

We have, to repeat, largely ignored this phenomenon of increased Jewish commitment on the part of a small proportion of college youth. If one despairs for the future survival of the mass of American Jews, then this small group is in the long run of enormous significance. But as long as one continues to define a Jew as one whose minimal identification or whose family's nominal identification is Jewish, the deeply involved represent, at best, straws in the wind.

7

JEWISH LIBERALISM*

We have explained American Jewish behavior as a response, a reaction, to both the American environment and the Jewish past out of which the American Jew emerged. So far in our analysis we have described this response in terms of the changes which it effected in the behavior, beliefs, and self-definitions of American Jews. But organisms, institutions, and peoples need not respond solely by adjusting themselves to their environment. They may also seek to change their environment. This chapter, and to some extent the next, seeks to demonstrate how Jews have sought to change the American political environment to make it harmonize with their basic values. The thrust of this chapter is that Jewish political liberalism is just such an effort—to bring America into accord with the basic values of Jews, though not necessarily (as will be clarified here) with the basic values of Judaism.

*I am indebted to Jacob Toury, of Tel Aviv University, and to Milton Himmelfarb for their comments on an earlier draft of this chapter. Some material in the chapter was drawn from my own survey of Jews in Washington Heights, New York. That study was supported by the Memorial Foundation for Jewish Culture. An analysis of the political aspects of the survey data was made possible with the help of the National Foundation for Jewish Culture. An earlier version of this chapter appeared in Donald Cutler, ed., *The Religious Situation 1969* (Boston: Beacon Press, 1969).

JEWS AS LIBERALS

The observation that Jews are political liberals is well documented. To be more precise, American Jews support liberal and left-of-center political candidates, policies, and parties in numbers and intensity disproportionate to their percentage of the population and to their social class.[1] This support for liberalism appears to be a distinctively group phenomenon, rather than the coincidence of a set of similar characteristics among Jews. In other words, Jews share many social characteristics that distinguish them from other groups. They are not only wealthier on the average than members of all but a few high-status Protestant denominations, but they are also more urbanized and better educated; their social elite are clustered in professional occupations rather than employed as executives of large corporations or financial institutions.[2]

Jewish liberalism, however, appears to be independent of these social phenomena. Campbell, Converse, Miller, and Stokes constructed six test groups that normally vote Democratic. They set up controls for such characteristics as current residence (region and size of community), past residence, education, occupation, income, age, generations in the United States, and other group memberships. They found that differences between some test groups and control groups virtually disappeared. Using the 1956 presidential vote as the index, the Catholic test group was only 2.9 percent more Democratic than the control group, and nonsouthern Negroes were 11.6 percent more Democratic. The highest differential they found was among the Jews, who were 45.4 percent more Democratic than would be expected from other social and demographic characteristics.[3]

Jews, however, do not support the Democratic candidates because of any special ties to the party. Campbell and Cooper found that Jews vote more heavily Democratic than any other religious group,[4] but that they were less likely than Catholics and no more likely than Protestants to consider themselves strong Democrats.[5] (Twenty-one percent of the Jews and Protestants and 23 percent of the Catholics considered themselves *strong* Democrats.) In contrast, 32 percent of the Jews, as compared to 27 percent of the Catholics and 25 percent of the Protestants, considered themselves *weak* Democrats; 18 percent of the Jews, as compared to 13 percent of the Catholics and 7 percent of the Protestants, considered themselves *independent* Democrats. Jews, however, were more aware of the political issues than Protestants or Catholics,[6] which reinforces my conviction that preference for the Democratic party is not attributable to Democratic partisanship. Indeed, the Jews' disproportionate support for the (Henry) Wallace Progressives in the 1948 presidential campaign suggests that it is issue orientation which motivates them.[7]

The political issues around which Jews mobilize are not primarily those concerning their own economic welfare. Survey Research Center respondents were asked whether it would make any difference in how their family managed financially if the Democrats or Republicans won. Campbell and Cooper found that despite the strong voting support of Jews for the Democratic party, only 18 percent of them, as compared to 21 percent of the Catholics and 22 percent of the Protestants, thought they would be better off if the Democrats won. In contrast, 15 percent of the Jews, 11 percent of the Protestants, and 10 percent of the Catholics thought they would be better off if the Republicans won.[8] In a study of selected wards in Boston, Fuchs found that Jews who supported Adlai Stevenson mentioned his liberalism as well as his personal qualifications as reasons for supporting him. Non-Jews stressed his party identification or the fact that he favored their economic group.[9]

Jews are not only less influenced by a candidate's party than are other groups, they are also less influenced by a candidate's religion. John F. Kennedy's Catholicism evoked a much more neutral response among Jews than among either Catholics or

Protestants in the 1960 presidential race.[10] This is also the case when the candidate is Jewish.

Robert Morgenthau, whose family has been very prominent in Jewish life, received the nomination for governor of New York State in 1962 on the basis of a poll which suggested that he would receive 82 percent of the Jewish vote and would run appreciably better among the Jews than would a Catholic or a Protestant, and without losing any normally Democratic Catholics or Protestants.[11] The predicted Jewish vote was inaccurate. Jews did not vote solidly for Morgenthau, and a poll completed a week before the election showed that as many as "50 per cent of New York City Jews who had voted for the Democratic candidate, Averell Harriman, in 1958, were undecided about voting for Morgenthau four years later."[12]

In 1962 the returns from seven predominantly Jewish districts showed Governor Nelson A. Rockefeller increasing his support over 1958 in six districts. In fact, Rockefeller's percentage of the two-party vote in these districts was uniformly greater in 1962 than was Jacob Javits's when Javits, a Jew, first ran for the United States Senate in 1956. Javits's vote in 1962 exceeded Rockefeller's, but even the substantial increase in Javits's support is significant. It suggests that his Jewishness alone was not enough to insure him support among Jews in his first campaign, and that he had to prove himself as a liberal.

In New York City it is difficult to mobilize Jews around a Jewish candidate even where only local issues are at stake. In the 1961 mayoralty primary, Robert Wagner, of German-Irish background but with reform backing, captured 63 percent of the vote in twenty-three predominantly Jewish election districts against his opponent, Arthur Levitt, a Jew running with the support of the Democratic organization. In the regular election, Jews continued to back Wagner against his Republican opponent, a Jew, Louis Lefkowitz.[13] In contrast, John Fenton found that not only do Catholics support Catholic candidates, but even "militant" Protestant denominations such as Lutherans and Southern Baptists discriminate in favor of a candidate of their own religion.[14] Given the intensity of their ethno-religious commitment, one might consider Jews equally militant and likely to favor a Jewish candidate. But apparently this is not the case, at least not to a noticeable extent. One can say that being Jewish is not among the qualities a candidate must have to attract Jewish support.

THEORIES OF JEWISH LIBERALISM

Jewish attraction to liberal or left-of-center policies and candidates, then, appears to be an orientation toward a liberal ideology or to a candidate whose style embodies the values of liberalism, or both. Three theories have been offered to explain this orientation. The first finds the basis for Jewish liberalism in religious values, the second finds it in the purported inferiority of the Jew's status, and the third is based on particular historical conditions.

Religious Values

Fuchs has suggested that at least a partial explanation for Jewish liberalism and internationalism rests on traditional Jewish standards.[15] He attributes their political attitudes to their values: respect for learning, individual and communal responsibility for the welfare of others (zedakah), and appreciation of life's pleasures (nonasceticism or this-worldliness). Learning, according to Fuchs, is translated politically into respect for intellectuals and intellectual independence (that is, civil liberties) and identification with the Democratic presidential candidates and their brain trusts (at least since 1932); another expression of this value is support of social planning, which the Democrats' cooptation of university scholars and intellectuals in government has generated. Charity (zedakah) is translated politically into support for welfare policies and social justice for underprivileged groups. Nonasceticism means that the Jews are concerned with a better life here and now, and favor reconstructing the present society rather than awaiting a heavenly reward.

It is difficult to test Fuchs's theories directly. He may be correct in assuming that Jewish liberalism finds its explanation in Jewish religious values, but he may be wrong about the values.[16] My concern is not so much with *which* religious values account for Jewish liberalism but rather with whether *any* religious values explain the phenomenon. In order to demonstrate that liberalism is accounted for by traditional religious values it is not enough to show that one can find values in the religious culture which promote liberalism; one would have to show that values which lead to political conservatism are absent in Judaism. Otherwise, all that could be said is that Jews are selective about their religious values, choosing or being influenced by only those that lead to liberalism. But in that case there is no theory, because the crucial question still remains: Why do Jews choose or why are Jews more influenced by the religious values which promote liberalism rather than those which promote conservatism?

The fact is that Jewish religious values are not unambiguously liberal; they are folk oriented rather than universalistic,[17] ethnocentric rather than cosmopolitan, and at least one major strand in the Jewish tradition expresses indifference, fear, and even hostility toward the non-Jew. One may assume that Jewish intellectualism and a belief in rational mastery of the world are outgrowths of a commitment to study and learning. The transfer from the study of Torah to the studies of other disciplines or to the belief in rationality is not an inevitable process. There was, for example, an anti-intellectual strain within Judaism at the folk level coterminous with the rise of Hasidism in the eighteenth century. But this strain was quickly submerged by the Hasidim themselves. More significantly, there has always been a strong antiphilosophical, antispeculative tradition in Judaism (though not the only tradition), and most of the Eastern

European religious leadership, particularly in the nineteenth and twentieth centuries, opposed secular education and the pursuit of any nontraditional Jewish study that was not value neutral. Furthermore, the traditional Jewish view of history and the reality perceptions of the traditional religious leadership to this day are quite removed from any notion of man's ability to master the universe rationally. Events were and still are viewed as the direct will of God, who often intervenes directly in the affairs of the universe, particularly when the well-being of Jews is at stake.

It is quite true that one can contrast the basic patterns of Judaism and primitive religion and find that Judaism, with its stress on transcendence, left an area of activity susceptible entirely to rational mastery by man.[18] But the living tradition of Judaism stressed that the prosperity and tribulations of the Jewish people were the result of God's rewarding or punishing them for their response to His commands dealing with personal conduct and ritual. The traditional Jewish responses to imminent threats of a pogrom were fasting, prayer, and appeals to the mercy of God, as much as any reliance on what today would be called rationally oriented activity. Characteristic of traditional Judaism is the anecdote told about the Arab attacks on Israel in 1948, when a religious Jew is supposed to have announced: "Jews! Don't rely on miracles, recite the psalms."

It is not at all clear, therefore, that the Jewish tradition unambiguously stresses secular study, intellectualism, and rational mastery of the world, all of which would lead to political liberalism. While Jewish liberals may find their source of values in the religious tradition, conservatives may do so too. At the least, each group is choosing selectively. Even if the tradition did stress only those religious values or beliefs that might lead to liberalism, however, one would still have to assume that theological values or beliefs are transferable to the political arena. This assumption is highly problematical in light of our knowledge that the political behavior of most groups tends to be rooted in specific notions of group or self-interest, or associated with particularistic values, rather than in the consequence of a diffuse ideology—particularly an ideology derived from theology.[19]

If Jewish religious values were exclusively liberal, and if one could assume a transfer from religious values or beliefs to political behavior, then one would expect those Jews who are more traditional or more religious to be more liberal. One test of whether Jewish religious values account for Jewish liberalism would be to test whether Jews who are more religious are in fact also more liberal.

But what exactly is meant by being religious? Sociologists of religion are convinced that religion is not unidimensional,[20] and they can identify a variety of religious dimensions. Those which have greatest currency in the study of religion include ritualism, the subjective experience of God, faith in the doctrines of one's religion, knowledge of one's religion, involvement with one's religious community, and the extent to which one feels his religion plays an important role in his life. In modern Judaism, more so than at any time in the past, and much more so than in Protestantism, all these dimensions are associated with one's particular denomination. By any of these criteria Orthodox Jews are more religious than Conservative or Reform Jews. Conservatives, in turn, are generally more religious than Reform in most of the dimensions for which data are available.

One of the most recent and carefully designed surveys of any Jewish community is a study of Boston Jews.[21] It reports that Orthodox Jews were more ritually observant than non-Orthodox Jews, were more likely to be members of Jewish organizations, were more likely to be affiliated with a synagogue and to attend services, and were likely to have had a more extensive and intensive Jewish education than non-Orthodox Jews. Most significantly, Orthodox Jews more than Conservative and Conservative more than Reform strongly oppose intermarriage, certainly the best single measure of group commitment. In a survey of first- and last-year rabbinical students at Orthodox, Conservative, and Reform theological seminaries, it was found that Orthodox students were more likely than Reform students to believe in a personal God to whom man can meaningfully pray, to believe in God's revelation, and to find prayer a significant personal experience.[22] In a survey to be discussed below, Jews in the upper portion of Manhattan who reported themselves as Orthodox were more likely to feel that religion plays a very important role in their lives than those who considered themselves Conservative or Reform.

Since Orthodox Jews seem to be consistently more religious than the non-Orthodox, it seems fair to test the religious-value theory by asking whether Orthodox Jews are more liberal than non-Orthodox Jews. If they are not, then we have reason to reject the theory that Jewish liberalism stems from Jewish religious values. There is no definitive study of the political behavior of groups within the Jewish community. What evidence there is suggests that Orthodox Jews are less liberal than non-Orthodox. However, unless social class—particularly education, which is so significantly related to political views—is a constant, comparisons are tricky. The data are, therefore, of a tentative nature.

Among American rabbinical organizations, the Reform preceded the Conservatives, who in turn preceded the Orthodox, in expressing a concern with social justice in the United States.[23] The only Jewish religious groups which expressed support for President Johnson's Vietnam policy were Orthodox lay and rabbinical organizations. A study of the opinions of American rabbis found that on issues involving economic welfare, civil liberties, peace, and internationalism, Orthodox rabbis were decidedly less liberal than Conservative or Reform rabbis.[24] In a study of Jews in Washington Heights (the upper portion of Manhattan), mailing lists of Orthodox synagogues formed the base for a mailed questionnaire.[25] Respondents were asked to classify themselves as Orthodox, Conservative,

Reform, or not religious. They were then asked a series of questions to measure their attitude toward government intervention in the economy, free speech, and the idea of Negroes as neighbors. With socioeconomic status (a combined measure of the respondents' income, occupation, and education) as a constant, the study found that Jews who classified themselves as Orthodox were consistently less liberal than those who classified themselves as non-Orthodox on all measures except attitudes toward Negroes.

Edgar Litt interviewed a sample of eighty Jewish males affiliated with Conservative synagogues in New Haven. They were all acculturated, second-generation Americans of East European background, living in the same area and of similar age, income, and occupation. He devised an Index of Ethno-Religious Involvement based on a series of questions concerning attendance at synagogue services, the use of Yiddish expressions, readership of the community's Anglo-Jewish magazine, activity in Jewish organizations, and participation in all-Jewish friendship cliques.[26] He found no relationship between ethno-religious involvement and political liberalism. Jews who were greater participants in the social, cultural, and religious life of the community and more steeped in its traditions were no more likely to be politically liberal than other Jews in the sample. This evidence seems to indicate that one cannot find the source of Jewish political liberalism in the religious values of Judaism.

Socioeconomic Factors

An alternative explanation for Jewish liberalism or leftist voting is based on the purported status inferiority of Jews. Those who take this position argue that Jews hold a social status far below what they might anticipate from their economic achievements. Consequently they are attracted to radical parties and political ideals which challenge the very political establishment and culture that deprives them. According to Seymour Lipset, "the leftist voting pattern of the Jews has been explained as flowing from their inferior status position (social discrimination) rather than from elements inherent in their religious creed."[27] There is no direct evidence to support this assertion; it is a hypothesis to account for Jewish deviation from the pattern which one might predict from a theory of socioeconomic causation.

Certain obvious problems arise with the status-inferiority theory. First, it accounts for Jewish radicalism rather than Jewish liberalism. While it is important to understand why Jews are found in parties of the radical Left in numbers far out of their proportion of the total population, it is not clear that this element is representative of Jewish tendencies.[28] The theory of status inferiority may explain the behavior of certain Jews, but it is not sufficient to explain the deviant behavior of most Jews, who are attracted to liberal left-of-center parties rather than to the radical Left. Second, the distinction we would draw between the radical Left and liberalism is that the radical Left provides a total ideology and demands a total commitment. Radical socialism is a substitute for Judaism; liberalism need not be. Given the conditions under which liberals and radical Socialists have lived, their peer groups, and their likely perceptions of their environment, it would be liberals more than radical Socialists who would suffer, or view themselves as suffering, from status inferiority. And to say that Jews were not radical Socialists in ideology but only voted for parties of the extreme Left is to account for party orientation, not issue or candidate orientation, which is the kind of theory required.

While the status-inferiority hypothesis, if correct, presents a general theory of some importance, it leaves unanswered the more specific question of interpreting Jewish response to the political environment: Why should the Jews respond to society's image of them rather than to their own self-image? Herein lies the answer to the greater liberalism of some Jews, particularly the nonreligious. They are precisely those who are most concerned with society's image, those for whom reality is defined by the values of the non-Jewish world. But liberalism to them is not a radical ethic, but an ethic which promotes acceptance.

The empirical literature provides no direct support for the theory of status inferiority, and in fact there is some evidence to the contrary. Litt also tested the relationship between political liberalism (tolerance and altruism) and feelings of ethnic subordination. Ethnic subordination was defined as "insecurity and defensiveness in social situations with Gentiles, and concern about recriminations for conspicuous Jewish behaviour."[29] Litt found that Jews who feel subordinate "are least likely to be tolerant of political nonconformists and altruistic toward other deprived groups."[30]

Historical Factors

The liberalism of Jews is also explained by relating to their particular historical condition. Werner Cohen traces Jewish liberalism to the experience in postemancipation Europe.[31] Following the French Revolution, the political Left propounded the view that only nationhood and not religious affiliation should determine citizenship. The conservative parties of the Right, however, associated citizenship with the older cultural traditions, which included Christianity. This excluded Jews from the parties of the Right, leaving them no alternative but to join the Left. Cohn notes that parties of the moderate Left were particularly congenial to Jews, since these parties not only defended them against conservatives but also upheld law and order against plebian attacks and revolutionary capriciousness, which often included anti-Semitic sentiments. The extreme Left attracted some Jews, however, because its political ideology, unlike that of the moderates, suggested a total way of life in which religious distinctions were irrelevant. Cohn goes on to discuss the impact of more contemporary events, concluding that American Jewish liberalism is sustained by the Jews' sense of insecurity in the gentile environment.

A problem arises with the historical theory: as an explanation it posits too much for a particular historical condition, and it fails to account for distinctions among Jews. Historical occurrences may certainly be relevant to contemporary behavior, but only if subsequent events reinforce, or at least maintain, conditions from the time they first occurred. If Cohn's historical theory is an adequate explanation, it is because there are certain constants in the postemancipation experiences and perceptions of the Jews. But it is these constants that must be considered.

In addition, even if the historical explanation is adequate, it is incomplete unless it accounts for differences among Jews. As Cohn himself notes, the Orthodox Yiddish press on New York's Lower East Side was Republican, not Democratic or Socialist, at the turn of the century.

Then, too, the historical argument begs the question of why the Jews desired emancipation in the first place, particularly when it threatened traditional religious and communal values. The evidence suggests that the traditionalist elements within the Jewish community were *not* in favor of emancipation, and that the breakdown of Jewish traditionalism through the values of secularism, nationalism, and universalism preceded emancipation rather than followed it.[32]

Finally, the historical theory is somewhat problematical because it would suggest strong party, rather than issue, orientation among Jews. But the Jewish attraction to the parties of the Left was because of Jewish liberalism, not because Jews internalized the ideologies of the parties of the Left and became liberal. A theory is needed to account for Jewish liberalism, not leftist party orientation.

The data from the New York sample also afford some test of the theory that Jewish liberalism today is accounted for by the European experience, in which parties of the Right were closed to the Jews. If this theory is correct, then Jews born or raised in Europe should be more liberal than those born or raised in the United States, where parties of the Right were open to the Jews. The historical conditions described by Cohn were true throughout Europe. However, an alternative was open to the Jews in Eastern Europe which was unavailable in Germany: the development of indigenous Jewish political movements. In some instances, particularly in the case of the Orthodox in Poland, the Jewish parties were allied with conservative rather than liberal political forces. Hence, if the historical theory is of contemporary relevance in New York, one would expect to find the German Jews the most liberal, the East Europeans next, and the American Jew the least liberal.

In the analysis, socioeconomic status and age were constants. On the question of governmental regulation of the economy, which is the most overtly political question and the least likely to be influenced by particular Jewish conditions, there was no consistent pattern by place of birth, although the Germans were generally the least liberal and the American-born the most, a pattern opposite to the one which was hypothesized. On the free-speech question one might suggest, contrary to Cohn's theory, that the European-born, particularly the Germans, would be least liberal in light of their experience from the Weimar Republic to Hitler. This was generally true, but the American-born were not significantly different from the East Europeans. Attitudes toward Negroes as neighbors showed no consistent patterns.

Liberalism and Group Ties

If Jewish liberalism emerges from a sense of Jewishness, whether religious or historical, a greater liberalism would be expected among those Jews whose involvement with Judaism is greatest. In their study of Elmira, Berelson, Lazarsfeld, and McPhee found that the more closely Jews identified with their group, the stronger their Democratic vote was.[33] Fuchs, how-

ever, in his study of selected wards in Boston, found that high
ethnic involvement did not account for Democratic voting,[34]
and Litt in his New Haven study found no significant relationship between ethno-religious involvement and political liberalism.[35]

Fuchs accounts for Jewish Democratic defectors by catego-
rizing them as Jews "who had the most frequent and extensive
contact with non-Jews in primary groups."[36] His evidence
shows greater Republican voting among Jewish men than Jewish women and among Jewish suburban residents than Jewish
city residents; he also found that Democratic candidates had
greater attraction for students at almost exclusively Jewish institutions (Brandeis and Yeshiva) than for a national cross-section
of Jews.

My own sample data support an extension of Fuchs's observations to include political values as well as to Democratic voting.
Respondents were asked about their organizational memberships in order to permit a comparison between those who belonged to more nonsectarian than Jewish organizations and
those who belonged to more Jewish than nonsectarian organizations. With socioeconomic status as a constant—except for attitudes toward having Negro neighbors, where there are no differences—those who belong to more Jewish than nonsectarian
groups are more liberal. So it appears that while Jewish liberalism is not supported by any particular sense of Jewishness or
Jewish commitment, it is reinforced by association with other
Jews.

A THEORY OF JEWISH LIBERALISM

One would now expect to find the source of Jewish liberalism
among the values of Jews who are somewhat estranged from
their religious tradition but associate primarily with other Jews.
This value lies in the search for a universalistic ethic to which
a Jew can adhere but which is seemingly irrelevant to specific

Jewish concerns and which, unlike radical socialism, does not demand total commitment at the expense of all other values.[37] The unique quality of Jewish voting and Jewish attitudes suggests that the explanation lies in the unique condition, experience, or values of the Jew, or of most Jews—which is not necessarily the same thing as Judaism. If no theory has sufficed, it is because none has explored the uniqueness of the Jewish situation.

However, Jewish liberalism must be more carefully defined. The basic Jewish commitment is not to a constellation of political policies (internationalism, civil liberties, and social welfare) which bear the name liberalism. Instead, it is to Enlightenment,[38] the optimistic faith that the application of human intellect can create a constantly progressing universal cosmopolitan society. Internationalism, libertarianism, and welfarism are consequences of this basic commitment. But it is the image of the enlightened society and the Enlightenment liberal that holds greatest resonance for the Jew. To this extent, political style may be more important than policy content. The East European Jewish immigrant had barely broken out of the caste of traditional society when he arrived in the United States. Commenting on these Jews in Boston one observer noted:

The Jew is a thorn in the flesh of the Irish politician. . . . At first the Jews so imperfectly understood the political game that they formed educational clubs to influence their people without regard to the party affiliations of prospective citizens. Such conduct is incomprehensible to Irish politicians.[39]

The Jewish vote for president in 1912 is instructive. Teddy Roosevelt earned a reputation as a friend of the Jews when he was police commissioner in New York and assigned only Jewish policemen to protect a German anti-Semite who came to New York to address a public meeting. As president, Roosevelt extended unusual courtesies to the Jewish people, appointed many Jews to public office, and pursued a philo-Jewish policy through his intervention in behalf of Jews persecuted in Russia. In 1904 he had the support of the majority of American Jews.

Nevertheless, in 1912 Woodrow Wilson "became the first Democratic Presidential candidate to crash the Republican hold over the Jews in half a century."[40] Jews deserted the Republicans—and particularly Teddy Roosevelt—because although Roosevelt had pursued a pro-Jewish policy, Wilson was the symbol of the political leader with whom Jews could identify: the college professor and idealist, not the Roughrider. This distinction is reflected in characteristic endorsements for each of the two men. In 1904 a major Anglo-Jewish weekly urged support for Teddy Roosevelt, arguing that while there ought not to be a Jewish vote, there was no reason for Jews not to vote for a man who "has indisputably done things that entitle him to the goodwill of our people."[41] In 1912, however, with Wilson in the race, another weekly announced that "Jews should support a man like him, who has made culture the shining purpose of his life."[42] Both Wilson and Roosevelt were liberals, but Wilson was the Enlightenment liberal, Roosevelt the more populist model.[43]

It is difficult to find instances of an Enlightenment candidate who is not particularly liberal opposing a substantive liberal who does not have an Enlightenment image. One such case may have been the Stevenson-Kefauver race for the Democratic presidential nomination in 1956. The two candidates met in a closely contested primary election in Florida.[44] Stevenson was the cultured, urbane candidate with a middle-of-the-road policy on domestic welfare and a surprisingly unsympathetic attitude toward Israel for a Democratic presidential candidate. Kefauver, with his coonskin cap and associated campaign style, had great appeal for the "Florida crackers." But he was also more liberal than Stevenson on economic matters and more favorable toward Israel. The heavy Jewish vote in the Miami area went to Stevenson. Only the militant Zionists and the Jews farthest to the Left supported Kefauver.

Jews do support Israel, of course. Despite the evidence, they simply could not conceive that Stevenson, the prototype of the Enlightenment candidate, could be anything other than pro-Israel. Jews are also economic liberals, but this is not a crucial issue. It is simply the sensible and reasonable position for an enlightened individual to take.

But for most Jews neither their economic liberalism nor even civil liberties has the emotional charge of the issue of church-state separation. Church and state, they feel, must be separate because otherwise two things will happen. First, the Catholic church will benefit, and the church, at least until a few years ago, was perceived as the major antagonist of reason, individuality, and personal freedom. Second, if religion is anything more than a private matter, Jews will be forced to assume a public identity as Jews. Thus Jewish separationist groups such as the American Jewish Congress are more militant in advocating church-state separation than liberal Protestant groups such as the National Council of Churches.

Enlightenment liberalism (that is, church-state separation) generally has greater resonance for most Jews than economic liberalism or welfarism. This can be seen in the campaign over New York State constitutional change in 1967. A constitutional convention in 1966 adopted a series of changes to be submitted to the voters in a single package. One change was interpreted as opening the door for state aid to religious schools. Other proposals liberalized welfare and state-aid requirements in a manner which would have benefited New York City and the poor. Most Republican leaders and the Conservative party denounced the proposed constitutional changes "as a spender's charter . . . as a 'bag of goodies' for New York City, and this theme was hammered home by Republican newspaper editors."[45] In New York City, however, the early fight against the constitutional changes was led by the "liberal" Jews, and the predominantly Jewish Liberal party. They were later joined by Protestant and good-government groups in opposition to the whole constitution because of its religious provisions. As Richard Morgan notes:

In vain a few voices warned that anti-social-welfare and anti-urban elements were mounting an unopposed scare campaign against the economic provisions of the proposed constitution. Preserving Blaine [the clause of the old constitution, omitted in the new one, which prohibited direct or indirect state aid to religious schools] was the issue of the hour for most of New York's liberal groups and leaders, and paralyzed those who were the natural enemies of economic conservatism. Within a matter of weeks opposition to the new constitution became a mark of liberal orthodoxy in the state.[46]

How, then, is one to explain the attraction of Enlightenment liberalism? If one looks at Jewish behavior since political emancipation, one sees two apparently contradictory phenomena. There appears to be a constant drive for the Jew to free himself from the condition which Judaism apparently thrusts upon him. This might be called the condition of estrangement. The impetus for intellectual and religious reform among Jews, the adoption of new ideologies and life-styles, and, above all, the changing self-perception by the Jew of himself and his condition were not simply desires to find amelioration from the physical oppression of the ghetto. They were a desire for emancipation from the very essence of the Jewish condition—being a member of a minority group different in quality and kind even from other minorities, and hence ineligible to participate, as other minorites did, as an equal member of society. This denial of equality was not simply a matter of rights. Even where the Jew was granted full political equality he still sensed his estrangement, indeed, often sensed it more acutely. The Jew's problem was his alienation from the roots and the traditions of the society. While the sense of estrangement is a constant throughout Jewish history, it was felt most sharply in the post-emancipation period where the gentile society and culture were no longer formally Christian, and secularization swept the

Jewish people, destroying traditional values. Thus these values no longer provided religious legitimation for the estrangement or assured the creation of a universal society in the messianic period. To the anti-Semite, the Jew, with his stress on universalism and intellect, threatens the traditional values and virtues of society.

The true Frenchman, rooted in his province, in his country, borne along by a tradition twenty centuries old, benefiting from ancestral wisdom, guided by tried customs, does not need intelligence. His virtue depends upon the assimilation of the qualities which the work of a hundred generations has lent to the objects which surround him; it depends on property. . . . He is the poet of real property. It transfigures the proprietor and endows him with a special and concrete sensibility. To be sure, this sensibility ignores eternal truths or universal values; the universal is Jewish, since it is an object of intelligence.[47]

While the Jew may not be able to understand a particular line by Racine, the Frenchman is able to say: "The way is open to me, mediocre me, to understand what the most subtle, the most cultivated intelligence has been unable to grasp. Why? Because I possess Racine—Racine and my country and my soil."[48]

The Jew always sensed his estrangement, but his perception of its nature underwent a secularization in the late eighteenth and early nineteenth century. This estrangement had been a condition of both physical and spiritual exile in which the Jew was alienated from a homeland and to some extent even from God—in which, indeed the spirit of God was itself alienated from the Godhead, a condition which could be resolved only through the physical and spiritual emancipation of a messianic era. After secularization, the Jew concerned himself with material and spiritual estrangement and alienation independent of its mystic religious context.

It is important to understand that secularization changed the nature of the Jew's perception of his condition, but many have not understood that secularization did not destroy the signifi-

cance of spiritual estrangement for the Jew. Rather, it transferred the realm of this spirit from its theological and mystical
concern to that of contemporary culture and civilization. Neither the new nation-state nor the Jew was satisfied with a
defined role for the Jews as a corporate entity. The barriers to
the individual Jew's participation in the society were ostensibly
removed, except that the new nation-states were building,
sometimes unconsciously, on the cultural traditions of the earlier Christian society. The Jew was really not prepared to accept
conditions for his participation in even secular society,[49] particularly as the non-Jew defined them: total surrender of Jewish
identity. Without such surrender the Jew remained an object of
suspicion. Jacob Toury notes that in the nineteenth century
Bruno Bauer, without ostensible national or racial bias, could
write about the Jews as follows:

All assertions, even by the most enlightened Jew, that he does not
envisage an independent nationality of "his people"—however sin-
cerely made—are illusory. . . . The Jew who in the present circumstances, with his enlightenment, and his social aspirations, still wants
to remain a Jew, he is the true Jew and exemplifies most clearly the
strength and verity of Judaism. . . . The emancipation of the Jews in
a radical and successful manner is only possible when they are to be
emancipated not as Jews, i.e. as beings that must always remain alien
to Christians, but when they [turn] themselves into human beings who
are not any longer kept apart . . . from their fellow humans.[50]

Toury observes that "the new acculturated and socially ambitious Jew, who nevertheless cannot be totally absorbed and does
not want to be totally absorbed, because he clings to an 'illusion'
of Jewry, constitutes the real 'Jewish question.' "[51]

But there were options open to the Jew. He could convert to
Christianity, and if his accent and life-style remained barriers
to his acceptance in the gentile society, at least his children
would be relieved of their Jewish disability. Yet remarkably few
Jews chose this alternative, or even the alternative of abandon-

ing all Jewish ties as a preliminary step to assimilation. Many of the overtly assimilated Jews, those who most consciously sought to uproot their own traditions and enter gentile society, continued to devote their efforts to assimilating other Jews, a strategy which can only be viewed as self-contradictory. From one perspective (though only a partial one) the problem of Jewish survival in the modern world has been compounded by the unwillingness of assimilated Jews to cut their ties with the Jewish community. Not only have they been unwilling to dissociate themselves from other Jews, they have even vied to lead them.

A secular ideology of a quasi-religious nature such as communism also provided a partial alternative. The Jewish Communists, according to Albert Memmi, are distinguished from non-Jewish party members by their more complete immersion into party activity and life. They seek to install themselves in the "warm bosom of the Party" and construct a "protected universe which cannot be penetrated by the hostility of the world." But

the Jew-of-the-Left must pay for this protection by his modesty and anonymity, his apparent lack of concern for all that relates to his own people. . . . Like the poor man who enters a middle-class family, they demand that he at least have the good taste to make himself invisible.[52]

Most Jews were not looking for an escape from Judaism. This is the other side of the Jewish predicament. When nothing else remained to give him a separate identity, when it appeared as though the Enlightenment millennium of a universal society open to the Jew had indeed come, he still sought a distinct identity, if in no other way than through affiliation with other Jews. Most Jewish Marxists in Poland were not Communists; they were Bundists. And, at least in the early 1920s, all that separated the General Jewish Workers Bund of Poland from the Communists was the Bundists' insistence on retaining their organizational identity.[53] The Jew sought the options of the Enlightenment but rejected its consequences. In the first instance he sought an ethic which cut across the older societal divisions.

Jews were enthusiastic supporters of universal humanism and cosmopolitanism. They embraced democratic nationalism, liberalism, and moderate socialism. There were variations from one region to another and one period to another. The Jews' response to their condition in Western Europe differed from that in Eastern Europe, and the American response differed from all others. There were different responses as well in the early nineteenth century, the late nineteenth century, the early twentieth century, and the post-World War II period. Nor did all Jews respond in quite the same way. What is striking, however, is the constant search for a universalistic ethic which would cut through the differences that an older tradition had imposed, but which would permit the Jew to retain at least nominal identification as a Jew.

The Jew desperately sought to participate in the society and rejected sectarianism as a survival strategy, yet at the same time refused to make his own Jewishness irrelevant. Actually, Judaism, with its religious particularism and cultural and ethnic overtones, is indeed not irrelevant to the extent that the new nation-state aspired to a uniform culture and civilization. The most the Jew was willing to do was redefine the nature of his commitment to Judaism and his perceptions of the content of Judaism, but he also sought a more congenial definition of society.

The Jew made and continues to make contradictory demands on society. He wants to be accepted into the traditions of society without adapting to the society's dominant tradition. Meanwhile, the Jew continues his search for an ethic or ethos which is not only universal or capable of universality, but which provides a cutting edge against the older traditions of the society, a search whose intensity is compounded and reinforced by the Gentile's treatment of the Jew.

Thus, certainly in America, the Jew chose liberalism not conservatism, cosmopolitanism not nationalism, an urban not a rural style. The Jewish political quest was for an ethic which could be posed against society's traditions. To this extent, then, the Jew sought to *Judaize* society. But this Judaization does not stem from intrinsic Jewish values. Of course, cosmopolitanism, universalism, liberalism, and even socialism can be found in traditional Judaism. But so can ethnic particularism, nationalism, and political conservatism. The modern Jew chooses that part of the tradition which is compatible with his special interests. He raises these interests to the level of ideology and presses them upon society in universalistic terms. The Jew thus fights for separation of church and state in the name of a secular ideal, not a Jewish ideal. From a parochial traditional Jewish point of view, one must be blind not to see the danger of secularization to Judaism. But the Judaization of society is not the quest to universalize Jewish values; it is the desire to impose the Jewish condition of estrangement upon society.[54]

I do not want to exaggerate the phenomenon of Judaization. The Jewish condition of alienation *is* shared by other groups, most notably the uprooted rural intellectual who identifies so readily with Jews and sometimes even calls himself an "honorary Jew." The difference, however, is that most "honorary Jews" learn that they really are not totally accepted into even the secularist humanist liberal company of their quondam Jewish friends. Jews continue to insist in indirect and often inexplicable ways on their own uniqueness. Jewish universalism in relations between Jews and non-Jews often has an empty ring; it expresses only one aspect, even though it is the increasingly ascending aspect, of the Jewish condition. Still, we have the anomaly of Jewish secularists and atheists writing their own prayer books. We find Jewish political reformers breaking with their local parties which stress an ethnic style of politics, and ostensibly pressing for universal political goals—while organizing their own political clubs which are so Jewish in style and manner that non-Jews often feel unwelcome.

Enlightenment liberalism, then, is a value which for the Jew has both universal and Jewish aspects. It is an effort to achieve universality for Jews, rather than for individuals. It is thus reinforced, not weakened, by those whose maximal contacts are with other Jews. Jews prefer to get together with other Jews to promote ostensibly non-Jewish enterprises (which assist Jewish acceptance) and then to pretend the whole matter has nothing to do with being Jewish. But this type of activity is most prevalent among Jews who are the most estranged from their own traditions and hence most concerned with finding a value that supports Jewish acceptance without overtly destroying Jewish group ties.

What of the future of Jewish liberalism in America? Its future is no more assured than is the continued state of Jewish estrangement. This estrangement depends in turn upon a number of factors: the ability of the Jew to redefine his religion and the nature of his commitment, the Jew's desire for survival, the non-Jew's terms for Jewish acceptance, the extent to which American society reflects its Christian experience, and the extent to which the Jew perceives anti-Semitism from the Left. My own impression is that the future of Jewish liberalism in America is a bleak one.

8

RADICAL JEWISH STUDENTS
AND THE JEWISH FAMILY*

Chapter 7 dealt with the efforts by American Jews to reshape their political environment in consonance with their basic values. The behavior of radical Jewish students might be viewed as a similar effort. But the differences are critical. Jewish liberalism reflects the values of integration and survival. What values do the Jewish campus radicals of a postliberal generation reflect?

In exploring the answer to this question we shall see that the youthful radicals differ from their liberal parents, not only in the basic values which their behavior manifests, but also in their orientation to these values. Jewish liberalism today, like Jewish radicalism of the past, is goal oriented. The current radicalism of Jewish students, we suggest, is less goal oriented and more an effort to act out certain conceptions of reality. These conceptions, however, feed on the contemporary nature of American Jewish life.

---

*After completing this chapter I read Richard G. Braungart, "Family Status, Socialization and Student Politics: A Multivariate Analysis," *American Journal of Sociology* 77 (July 1971):108–30. Braungart's conclusions reinforce my own impressions. After presenting his findings he recommends "that future inquiry should focus on the value-orienting factor of parents' religious affiliation as it affects patterns of family socialization, while further investigation might also be undertaken as it influences the intensity and direction of student political activism." In retrospect, that is what this chapter is all about.

Of course, no simple or single explanation can account for the activism and militancy of many American college students during the past few years. Any total answer must involve education, politics, sociology, economics, philosophy, psychology, biology, and perhaps others. We want to know the condition of American universities and the particular conditions on the campuses where the more militant protests occurred. We must know something about the general political conditions in the United States and the development of radical ideology in its post-Bolshevik or post-1930 stage. We want to know something about the process of youth and maturity in the United States and the biological, social, and psychological processes through which individuals pass during a certain period of their lives. We want to know the educational, social, and familial backgrounds out of which these young people come and their perception of the social and economic conditions that await them after college. But there is a particularly Jewish dimension to student unrest. As we shall see, student radicals are not only disproportionately Jewish, they represent a special type of Jew.

The high incidence of Jews among student radicals has been substantiated by a number of studies. In a study of student attitudes on the Berkeley campus of the University of California, Robert Somers classified his respondents into militants, moderates, and conservatives—depending upon whether they supported the goals and tactics, the goals but not the tactics, or neither the goals nor the tactics of the 1964 police-car demonstrators. During that demonstration, which led to the formation of the Free Speech movement and increased militancy on the part of some students, activists sought to prevent the arrest of students and their removal from the campus by the police. The study found that Jews were the most likely to be militants.[1]

In a comparision of activists and nonactivists at the University of Chicago, using data gathered in 1965 and 1966, Richard Flacks found that the activists "are far more likely to be Jewish than are the non-activists."[2] Flacks and others also found that "formal religion was not important or even relevant to the lives of most of the activists,"[3] both Jewish and non-Jewish. This finding for Jews is reinforced by the interesting study of students participating in a Free Speech movement sit-in at Berkeley, who were compared to a random sample of Berkeley students. The proportion of Protestants and Catholics participating in the sit-in was lower than each group's proportion in the sample of the total student population. Jews and those who professed no religion constituted a higher proportion of the demonstrators than their proportion of the total student sample. But the disproportionate number of students who identified themselves as Jews was not statistically significant. By contrast, the disproportionate number of students who reported that their mother was Jewish was significantly greater than the proportion who reported that their mother was Protestant or Catholic.[4] In other words, the proportionately largest segment of student radicals were Jews (by birth) who no longer identified themselves as such.

In addition to being disproportionately Jewish and nonreligious, activists are likely to come from families which are urban, highly educated, professional, affluent, politically liberal, and permissive.[5] These characteristics are themselves not simply incidental to being Jewish but are related to traditional Jewish values and behavior as they were reshaped through the American experience. Other studies have suggested that the socioeconomic status of the Jews, their clustering in large urban centers, their penchant for education, their attraction to the professions, and their political liberalism are not matters of chance or coincidence but are related to the fact of being Jewish.[6] We wish, however, to pay particular attention to the two remaining characteristics of student activists as these are related to their Jewishness: the fact that they come from permissive homes and that both they themselves and their families are likely to be irreligious.

THE "PERMISSIVE" FAMILY

Some interesting theories have been advanced to account for the very close relationship between mother and child in the Jewish family. In the traditional Jewish family the woman's role was fulfilled through her bearing and raising of children. Martha Wolfenstein, for one, has suggested that traditional Jewish life erected strong defenses against sexual impulses.[7] This extended to the husband's attitude toward his wife and their mode of sexual relations after marriage. The wife, never fully gratified through relations with her husband, tended to find a greater emotional outlet through her children. But the children, in turn, were taken from her at the age of three or four when they began their formal schooling. Thus the mother's perception of her child and their relationship, which was intense to begin with, became fixated in the preoedipal phase when the child is passive rather than active. This might explain the Jewish mother's constant and sometimes obsessive preoccupation with feeding and clothing her child. Furthermore, this also explains the mother's paradoxical perception of her child as powerless against the world, on one hand, but as capable of controlling *her* because of her great emotional investment and dependence on him, on the other hand.

One does not have to go all the way with Wolfenstein or similar theorists to agree with the phenomenon they are describing. As Marshall Sklare has pointed out,[8] despite the transformation of the traditional Jewish family in America, the parents continue to emphasize *extension* rather than *distinction* in their relationships with their children. Anything that happens to the child also happens to the Jewish parent. The child is of course a child, that is, weak and foolish; whereas the parent is an adult, that is, strong and wise. But the child's very weakness becomes a source of strength because he cannot be held entirely accountable for what he does. On the other hand, the child's strength in the power structure of the family is further enhanced by the parents' dependence on the child as their extension. He is, in the traditional folk formulation, their *nachas* (pleasure). Just as his success and achievements become theirs, so his failure reflects upon them.

It is the child, then, not the parent, who is independent. The parents, in turn, seek to protect themselves against this vulnerability by what outsiders call "spoiling" the child, but doting Jewish parents call "giving the child advantages." Sklare suggests that Gentiles view the Jewish permissiveness as "spoiling" because in the Anglo-American tradition they are typically so much less dependent on their children and hence so much less vulnerable to them. It would perhaps be more accurate to characterize the parent as "bribing" rather than "spoiling."

The economic and social consequences of this Jewish parent-child relationship are obvious—the willingness of children, for example, to move their place of employment away from their kin without a sense of having somehow betrayed their family. It is the parents, after all, who must give, and the children who receive.

The "old culture" Jewish pattern involved separations for business and educational reasons and a heightened consciousness that a man's first responsibility was for his children. That is, obligations were primarily from those that have more to those that have less, which practically speaking meant that children need not always stay to nurture parents who might be better off than they were.[9]

One might suggest that the same culture which permits the child to move spatially from his parents without a sense of his violating his responsibilities or obligations might also permit the child to move ideologically. The son may become more radical than his parents, and indeed may turn his radicalism against some institutions which the parents support, without the sense that this constitutes a turning against the parents themselves. "My revolutionary helped me plant those tulips last November, my rebel," Mrs. Rudd is quoted as saying about her son, Mark

Rudd, the head of the Columbia SDS chapter and leader of the 1968 student demonstrators there.[10] According to the *New York Times*, she speaks with "motherly pride" about her son. Rudd, in turn,

speaks of his parents with respect and affection, and they maintain that they are "100 per cent behind him," even though they don't agree with all his views. On Mother's Day last weekend [during the riotous period at Columbia] his parents went to the Columbia campus and brought a veal parmigiana dinner, which the family ate in their parked car on Amsterdam Avenue.[11]

Parental sympathy for the political radicalism of a son is particularly likely among student activists' families, among whom, as we noted, parents tend to be more politically liberal than parents of nonactivists.[12] Flacks, in his study of student activism, has suggested that students are involved in neither conversion to nor rebellion against their fathers' political perspectives, but rather that "the great majority of these students are attempting to fulfill and renew the political traditions of their families."[13] But if the permissive and liberal homes from which the students come are characteristically Jewish, this is not true of all the values of their homes. Nevertheless, even these other value patterns may be understood as the confluence of certain latent characteristics of the Jewish home: permissiveness, coupled with irreligion and marginality of the activists' families to the Jewish community.

Flacks has suggested four value patterns expressed by activists and their parents. The parents, who are predominantly second-generation Americans,[14] share with their children the values of, first, esthetic and emotional sensitivity—a concern with immediate and inner experience rather than the rational, technological, or instrumental side of life; second, a concern with ideas and participation in intellectual activity; third, a concern for others in society and a desire to help them, particularly the disadvantaged; and fourth, little concern about the importance of strictly controlling personal impulses or adherence to conventional authority and morality.

Now the second and third values, as we suggested in chapter 7 are broadly shared by American Jews and in fact are part of the Jewish tradition. Aesthetic and emotional sensitivity, which Flacks calls "romanticism," was also part of traditional Jewish life, but it was inwardly directed. In the traditional Jewish family, expressive needs were directed within the home and the Jewish community. One related to the gentile world primarily in economic terms, and one did so impersonally and instrumentally. The communal-social-religious realm of one's life, which excluded the non-Jew, was where one permitted a certain emotionalism to reign. But in his relations to the gentile world, the Jew was constantly on guard. Anything other than instrumental or impersonal relationships perforce meant the acknowledgment of one's Jewish identity and hence one's disability.

Of course, this approach to economic life made Jews readily adaptable to an economic system stressing contractual relationships and impersonality. It no doubt contributed to the rapid economic rise of the Jew in the United States. The economic success, the loss of Jewish identity, and the decline of Jewish sensitivity to perceived anti-Semitism meant that some second- and more third-generation Jewish Americans now relate to their non-Jewish environment in expressive terms. We must recall that we are dealing with a sample to whom religion is irrelevant—precisely that group whose strong expressive needs cannot find an outlet within the narrower Jewish community because they are not part of that community.

Jewish student activists, in the opinion of most observers, are not Jewish self-haters. They have, indeed, reached the zenith of assimilation. Judaism is so irrelevant to them that they need not even bother to deny their Jewish ancestry. A former student at Yeshiva College who always wears a yarmulke or skullcap, which identifies him as both Jewish and Orthodox, reported in private conversation an interesting experience when he visited SDS students at Columbia. Most overtly identifiable Jews who find themselves in a mixed environment of Jews and Gentiles where not everyone knows one another will invariably be approached by other Jews, often covertly, who seek to establish a Jewish contact—more often than not by hints and innuendo. If circumstances require a conversation between two individuals, both of whom are Jewish but each of whom is unsure of whether the other is Jewish, they are again likely to bring the matter up cautiously and indirectly until they are sure of each other's identity. Further, the style, though not the content, of the conversation is likely to be shaped by this knowledge. The conversants may be sufficiently (though never totally) conscious of this to be embarrassed by the sudden appearance of a non-Jew. The student was, therefore, surprised to find that for the first time in his life, his yarmulke and his Jewishness seemed totally irrelevant to any other Jew in his discussions with student activists during the tumult at Columbia.

The Jewish activist, as we noted, does not recognize the distinction between Jew and non-Jew. Indeed, this lack of recognition is itself a romanticization of reality implicit in the value pattern we previously discussed. The activist reshapes his perception of the environment to suit the perception of his utopia. Thus although a member of the *New York Times* editorial staff reported in a speech to the American Jewish Committee that the Columbia disturbances were breeding anti-Semitism[15] and some Columbia faculty privately expressed the fear that student demonstrations in which Jews played such a role would result in limitation on the future admission of Jewish students, student activists seemed totally unaware of any possible consequences that their activity might have for the Jewish community. While I have no evidence, it is believed by many at Columbia that a few years ago the university adopted a policy of limiting the number of Jews who could enter the undergraduate college. It did so by establishing quotas for students by geographical area. This served to handicap Jewish applicants who are clustered in the large urban centers, particularly those of the northeast. It is of some significance, therefore, that among the many sins of which the student militants accused Columbia University, not once (at least publicly) did they mention this discriminatory policy.

The irrelevance of Judaism, the absence of fear of anti-Semitism, permits the generalized expression of emotional feeling on the part of the activists. But the particular reflection of the loss of typically Jewish restraint is in the fourth value pattern which Flacks suggests as characterizing both activists and their families. This is the *low concern* with "the importance of strictly controlling personal impulses—opposition to impulsive or spontaneous behavior—value on keeping tight control over emotions—adherence to conventional authority . . . value on diligence, entrepreneurship, task orientation, ambition."[16] Here we find the ultimate Americanization of the Jews. On one hand, his ethnocentric image of the Gentile as imprudent, irrational, and nonintellectual was shattered by the reality of the non-Jew in America. This in turn contributed to a modification of the Jews' own sense of separatism and self-esteem and the diminution of community ties. On the other hand, the very success and mobility of the Jew, coupled with the loss of traditional values, transformed the Jew's own orientation toward authority and duty.

Work as a means to sanctity was transformed into work as a means to pleasure.[17] Self-gratification now became a legitimate pursuit to the acculturated Jew, particularly when the content of such gratification, as in the case of student activists, was consistent with other value standards of the home.

The students' failure to distinguish between a Jewish and non-Jewish world as the proper forum for different types of activity is related to an even grosser distinction that students fail to make—that between family and nonfamily.

The sense of the permissive, nourishing, all-giving family is easily transferred to the elementary and high schools in the upper-middle-class, heavily Jewish suburbs from which so many of the activist students come. The students, higher in measured intellectual disposition and intellectuality to begin with,[18] are rewarded for their originality and nonconformity in both home and school. Such students have a particularly low tolerance for frustration, seldom if ever encountering it either in their home or early school. There is a striking contrast between the bright American Jewish students' ready mastery of their high school curriculum and the Jewish student who receives a more traditional East Euopean yeshiva education with its stress on Talmud. Such a student experiences continual hardship and frustration in his study; no amount of diligence, study, or repetition ever seems sufficient to permit him, on his own, to resolve all problems satisfactorily.[19]

The self-gratification of the American student, to the extent that it has an intellectual orientation, is not only self-rewarding but in turn rewards both the family and the school. Admission to a school such as Columbia may certainly appear to such a young man as the ultimate favor he can bestow on his family and high school. Indeed, the attitude of his family and school to his college admission confirms that impression. Thus at no point in his academic life has the student felt any dissonance between home and school. His parents or friends' parents, no doubt active on school boards, PTAs, and the like, will further enhance the transfer of familistic orientations to school orientation. Why, then, should the student have a different set of expectations toward his university, which is also perceived as an extension of the family?

This suggests the answer to one small but troublesome question. Why have student activists expressed such surprise at the university's threat to expel or otherwise discipline them for their activity? How did they expect the university to treat them? The answer lies in the students' perception of their school. One may come home "after hours" on Saturday night, refuse to help mother do the dishes, break a window, or for that matter urinate on the carpet, but one is hardly expelled from the family for doing so. One can never be expelled from a family; that is one difference between their Jewish home and a university which some students are learning quite painfully.

In the students' minds, they had explained to the family-university or to the father-president that what the school was doing was wrong. They explained that limitations on free speech, not giving students enough voice in policy-making, not recruiting more Negro students, not opposing the war in Vietnam, building a gymnasium in Harlem, and so on were wrong. They were wrong by commonly accepted urban, intellectual, middle-class (Jewish) standards of right and wrong. The family-university refused to change its policy, or at least showed no signs of doing so instantly. Obviously, then, the only recourse left to the students was to escalate the pressure on the university. The alternative, acknowledging defeat, was simply unthinkable and probably immoral in the students' eyes. In the students' perception, the university brought the trouble on itself by refusing to do what it surely knew was right.

Thus, there is some question as to how much the students believed they were staking in their demonstrations and sit-ins. To some it may appear as though they were staking everything. To the students, the stakes may have been no higher than those involved in a confrontation with one's parents. In a study biased in favor of the more activist members of the Free Speech movement at Berkeley, Glen Lyonns found that at the time of the police-car demonstration, when police were prevented from making an arrest by students, only 7 percent of the demonstrators thought there was a good chance they would be expelled for their activity, and 22 percent said they felt there was a fair chance.[20] Significantly, a much higher proportion thought they were risking arrest by acting "illegally" on the Berkeley campus, but few thought they would be expelled for violating university regulations. Even those militants who felt they risked arrest were apparently not fearful of physical violence to their own persons.

Perhaps this same attitude explains the students' shock at the so-called police brutality at Columbia. I say "so-called" without denying the obvious fact of police shoving, dragging, clubbing, kicking, and beating students, faculty supporters, and even some bystanders, and without defending the police action. Rather, the term "so-called" should remind us that one man's brutality may be another man's normal arrest procedure. White middle-class students are simply unaccustomed to being pushed around, dragged, or clubbed by anyone, much less by the friendly neighborhood policeman who represents safety, security, and a public servant to upper-middle-class suburbanites.

But one can still fairly ask: How else did the students expect the police to behave? Given their rhetoric of radicalism, they certainly should have anticipated repression by the Establishment. But the very real shock of most activists and faculty supporters, though probably not the leaders, suggests that their condemnation of the university as an instrument of a corrupt Establishment was indeed only rhetoric. The students were shocked when Columbia called the police because middle-class families don't appeal to outside agencies to solve domestic problems. Negro demonstrators, who segregated themselves from the whites, anticipated police violence and were careful to avoid provocations. The whites, however, were shocked when the police handled them impersonally (not at all the way middle-class bright young men and women should be handled) because their own relationship to the total society, their "real" identity, was challenged. One need not have read the classic treatises on anarchy and violence to appreciate that what happened at Columbia should have profound implications for the student movement in redefining a new and truly radical identity for some and in separating out the moderate liberals, who may deplore the Establishment but are now more conscious of the real stakes and investment they have in the present system. It also suggests the likelihood that the next few years may see a proportionate decrease in white, as opposed to black, student militantism.

If this analysis is correct, and it is certainly far too impressionistic to be asserted as conclusive, it also suggests the chasm which separates the student activists of the 1960s from the Jewish campus radicals of the 1930s. The Jewish radicals of the depression period were second-generation, not third-generation, American Jews. They came from places like City College, not Columbia. They had less of a stake in the system and few illusions about the nature of the university. In more ways than one, the world was not their oyster. They were accustomed to hard work, discipline, and frustration, at least in the economic world. Even plebian City College was not an extension of their family, much less patrician Columbia.

Radicalism may have provided a substitute for and escape from the Jewish community, which they rejected as philistine, bourgeois, and inhibiting, but this rejection was self-conscious. Anti-Semitism would not have surprised them. They might have believed that it would find resolution in a confrontation with the existing social order or destruction of it, but the problem did, in one way or another, require a resolution. Most significantly, their radicalism was directed against the social order, not the university.

This is quite different from the perceptions of today's Jewish militant students. Ironically, their own activism may precipitate the very anti-Semitism whose reality they deny and which denial is itself a factor in their militant behavior.

Meanwhile the postliberal posture of the radical Jewish activist reflects the fact that he is untroubled by the tensions of survival and integration. Both values have lost resonance because they no longer seem necessarily desirable, or because they are assumed as a condition of life. The recurrence of anti-Semitism the past few years and the resurgence of ethnic particularism among non-Jews suggest that the radical-activists misjudge their environment. The extent to which changing events will lead to changing perceptions of reality and consequent changes in values remains to be seen.

PART THREE:

Conclusion

9

SOME OBSERVATIONS ON THE FUTURE OF AMERICAN JUDAISM

Will Judaism survive in the United States? This problem has the quality necessary for any intriguing question: it admits of no answer. Indeed, the mind boggles at even the notion of systematically outlining the dimensions of the solution or recording the assumptions that would have to be made in order to attempt a comprehensive answer. We are not so ambitious. But we can at least talk around the problem, utilizing the question for heuristic purposes—as a handle to outline a few of its dimensions, pausing along the way to treat one aspect or another at greater leisure.

We first note that Jews find great fascination in the question of whether Judaism in America will survive. This reveals both the strength and weakness of American Judaism. Weakness is implied in the doubt which the question suggests. Strength is implicit in the fact that those who pose the question assume that survival is a positive value. One would be less sanguine about Judaism's prospects if, instead of asking "Will Judaism survive," Jews asked whether it was worthwhile for Judaism to survive. Anyone who can seriously pose such a question to himself is unlikely to answer that survival is worthwhile. A will to live is an ultimate end. If group survival is cognitively recognized as merely an instrument to other ends, one is already predisposed to a negative answer.

CRITERIA FOR SURVIVAL

Let us return to our question: Will Judaism survive in the United States? We must first be clear as to what is meant by the survival of Judaism. The definition we will adopt here is the continuation of a set of practices, beliefs, and attitudes which have been associated with the Jewish people throughout their long history. Now we come to the rub. Even the most traditional Jew would agree that Judaism today is not identical with the Judaism of two thousand or one thousand or even one hundred years ago. Nobody denies that Judaism has changed. The question, then, is by what criteria do we determine whether a set of practices, attitudes, and beliefs that has undergone a change is still to be considered Jewish? If we could be transported to a future time of fifty or one hundred or a thousand years from now, how would we determine whether Judaism had or had not survived? It is at this point that some basic differences within the Jewish community are reflected.

The Orthodox Position

The first position we wish to consider is the one we label Orthodox. It is, in fact, identified with an Orthodox elitist position, although one conceivably can be Orthodox without subscribing to this position.

The Orthodox point of view is that in the absence of any new revelation, Judaism is essentially that which its talmudic masters or rabbinical authorities accept as authoritative. Judaism is seen in its essence as a system of legal practices and as a set of beliefs. The practices and beliefs are defined by rabbinical leaders of each generation, who authoritatively interpret scripture and codes to meet the exigencies and problems of each age.

Now, this position itself admits of many variations and view-points. For example, there may be differences of opinion about who the authoritative leaders are. While all Orthodox Jews agree that they must be masters of the Talmud, all Orthodox Jews do not accept the same talmudic masters as authoritative leaders. The latter, in turn, sometimes differ in their interpretation of Jewish law. In addition, the Orthodox position admits of differences in the extent to which the masses of Jews, or the needs of the time, or purely subjective considerations influence the decisions of its authoritative leaders. All Orthodox Jews would agree that their leaders do not simply manipulate the law to suit the proclivities of one group or another; nor do they simply function as representative legislators to enact the will of the people. But by the same token, these leaders are more than judges who mechanically apply a set of facts to a written code in order to determine right or wrong. To continue the analogy to judges, there is disagreement among the Orthodox about the extent to which their leaders do and should behave in an activist or restraining capacity.

Despite these differences, the Orthodox position does provide a ready technique for determining the legitimacy and therefore the *Jewishness* of a set of practices or beliefs. We need only ask the question: Has this or that practice or belief been sanctioned by the authoritative interpreters of Jewish law?

If we apply this criterion to contemporary American Jewish life we find that most nominally religious institutions in the United States are not Jewish, or perhaps we should say not Judaic. Their members are Jewish by Orthodox standards, but their practices are not. To put it another way, whereas Conservative and Reform Jews are indisputably Jewish by Orthodox standards, Conservative Judaism and Reform Judaism are not. Orthodoxy would have to argue, therefore, that if American Jewry was composed entirely of Conservative and Reform Jews, we would have Jews but no Judaism. Now, the reader should bear in mind that we have defined a position as Orthodox, and we are now following this position out to its logical conclusion. In actual fact the majority of Orthodox rabbis would not put the matter as we have stated it. That is because their own conception of Judaism is so intertwined with ethnic and communal overtones that Jews without Judaism are inconceivable. But the logical deduction from their own definition of Jewish authenticity does lead to this rather farfetched conclusion.

At this point one might demur and say: "You are creating artificial difficulties by insisting on discussing the problem of the survival of *Judaism;* why not focus on the question of the survival of the *Jews?"* If that is the question, then perhaps the Orthodox criteria are basically in harmony with the present nominally Jewish community. Unfortunately, that is not so. The Orthodox criteria are in some cases too narrow and in most cases too inclusive for the presently constituted Jewish community. On one hand, it excludes individuals born of non-Jewish mothers but raised as Jews who for one reason or another were never officially converted but who identify themselves with and are viewed by others as Jews. On the other hand, the Orthodox definition of a Jew includes some Episcopalians, probably quite a few Quakers and Unitarians, and countless Ethical Culturalists and atheists, none of whom identify themselves in any way with the Jewish community or are so identified by that community. As we noted in chapter 1, the traditional definition of a Jew includes ethnic as well as narrowly religious criteria. One who is born of a Jewish mother is a Jew, regardless of what he subsequently does. Thus by Orthodox criteria there are always likely to be Jews in the United States. To discuss the possibility of their survival, however, is pointless. One can only fruitfully discuss the question of the survival of Judaism.

There are, as we have already suggested, some problems with the Orthodox criterion, which leads to a denial of Judaic legitimacy to the religious institutions with which a majority of American Jews are identified. On the other hand, recent historical scholarship has suggested that in both ancient Palestine and

Babylonia many practices within the synagogues lay outside of normative Judaism.[1] Throughout Jewish history only those Jewish practices sanctioned by the authoritative interpreters of the law survived, no matter how small the number of Jews who originally adhered to them. The quantitative difficulty in Orthodoxy's criterion is, therefore, not insurmountable.

But there is a more serious problem. The problem is not with what Orthodoxy affirms or denies but with what it leaves unsaid. Its interpretation of Jewish authenticity makes irrelevant the most essential components of contemporary Jewish identity. The problem with the Orthodox criterion is not that it defines so much of American Judaism as unauthentic, but that it defines so much of American Judaism as irrelevant. As we have sought to show in this volume, Jewish identity in America includes, among its other aspects, a sense of social intimacy with other Jews; a sense of identification or attachment to the State of Israel as a political entity; a sense that anti-Semitism, however remote, always constitutes a threat; a sense that Jewish well-being is interrelated with Enlightenment, rationalism, social justice, political liberalism, and the separation of church and state; and a sense that Jews share a common history. Now, if all of these attitudes or sentiments were transformed to the cognitive level they might well be incompatible. In fact, as we have suggested, the very nature of American Judaism may be defined by the efforts to overcome mutually exclusive sentiments and beliefs. Furthermore, not all of these attitudes are rooted in the Jewish tradition, and some may even be antithetical to it. No one, therefore, argues that in the absence of one or more of these sentiments one could not be a Jew. But one could argue that if the Orthodox criterion for the establishment of Jewish authenticity simply does not speak to any of these major modes of identity, either affirming or denying them, then its categories for determining Jewish authenticity run the risk of becoming trivial. Orthodoxy's problem, then, is not what it says, but what it is silent about.

Orthodoxy is silent for a very good reason. The major categories for the expression of and determination of Jewish authenticity have always been legalistic, but the primary modes of Jewish expression today simply do not fit these categories.

We can put the matter another way. Rabbinical leaders are quite capable of responding to questions of "can I" or "am I permitted," or "must I." Such questions can elicit legal responses which are available, directly or indirectly, from the exegesis of sacred texts. What the authoritative Orthodox system is less able to cope with are, ironically, questions which involve basic orientations. Should I serve in Vietnam? Should I support the State of Israel? Should I socialize with non-Jews? Should I give my children a broad secular education?

Now, as long as the Jewish community bore the characteristics of a traditional society, such questions were not troublesome. In the first place, in traditional society the basic orientations are either assumed or are resolved within a communal rather than an individual framework. Moreover, prior to emancipation, Jewish secular authority was never divorced from religious authority. Indeed, secular authority bore the stamp of religious legitimation. Thus a religious solution could be found in terms of communal and social needs, as reflected in secular legislation. But in modern society, with its stress on the individual as an autonomous person and with the divorce of religion and state, institutional religion is called upon to exercise a far more critical and judgmental role. Those who turn to religion as a source of ethical or moral imperatives do so precisely because the activity of a secular state raises moral questions, and its authority lacks sufficient legitimacy to compel voluntary obedience. Paradoxically, at this critical juncture the rabbinical authorities cannot suggest solutions.

There is a third type of question that religious authority was also once able to answer: questions of "how," questions requiring technical competence in nonritualistic or legalistic fields.

This area of authority has long been surrendered by Jewish religious leaders except among certain Hasidic groups.

Orthodox leaders have been charged with a failure to speak out on many social issues. The charge may be true but it is unfair. In adapting themselves to the conditions of the nation-state, Jewish authorities necessarily circumscribed the areas to which Jewish law would be extended. But with the loss of Jewish corporate status, problems affecting Jewish identity and Jewish life could no longer be transformed into a legal framework. In addition, with the secularization of Jewish life or the neutralization of basic areas of Jewish experience from a previous Jewish mold, the rabbis lost the essential mechanism, both coercive and noncoercive, for imposing their values or decisions on the community.

If Orthodoxy was to survive, if its leaders were to retain any authority or exercise any influence, they had to adapt to the conditions of a secular world and a nation-state. They can hardly be condemned for adapting by delimiting their own area of competence to the more narrowly ritualistic. But modes of Jewish identity did not become concomitantly limited. If Jewish experience had limited itself entirely to areas of ritual and belief, then the rabbis could have continued as the sole arbiters for the legitimation of Jewish life. No doubt many Jews would have resisted their authority. But analytically this would not matter. If Jews were only Orthodox, Conservative, or Reform, then it would make sense for the Orthodox to argue "We are right and they are wrong." The trouble is that Orthodoxy, Conservatism, and Reform represent only one aspect of Jewish identity for most Jews, particularly for Conservatives and Reform Jews. It is a very small aspect in the Jewish lives of most American Jews, but it is the only one about which Orthodox leaders speak authoritatively. Most Jews, on the other hand, continue to express their Jewishness through a host of political, social, and cultural activities which rest outside the focus of rabbinical leaders.

Thus the conditions of modern society increasingly pose new

problems which lie outside the categories of Jewish law, as that law is understood today. This, in turn, has led to the charge that the rabbinical leaders are irrelevant. Such a charge denies the autonomy of the religious life even in its narrowest sense, as a self-legitimating mode of experience. The fact is that to many Jews, as to non-Jews, the religious life provides a most meaningful and satisfying experience. Within a Jewish context it is unfair to deny that to tens of thousands of people the most meaningful part of their lives comprises acts of worship, eating ritually permitted food, fasting, and, preeminently, the study of sacred texts. These activities depend, directly or indirectly, on the continuing exercise of religious authority by talmudic masters. Charges of irrelevance tend to come from the liberal segments of the religious community. One might counter with a charge that these elements lack sufficient religious sentiment and sensitivity to comprehend the legitimacy of an autonomous religious experience. But it does not answer the charge that Orthodox leaders do not speak for other basic realms of Jewish experience.

Now, proponents of the Orthodox point of view might argue that its leaders have the right not only to determine what is or is not Jewishly right, but also what does or does not constitute Jewish experience. At this point, however, those who so argue stand in a very ambiguous position to the Jewish tradition. If the only way that the tradition itself may be manipulated is by denying the relevance of the strongest feelings and sentiments of Jews to Judaism, it is hard to see how the tradition can survive or how it can command assent from even the most traditional Jews.

To most Orthodox Jews the objections raised here are hardly compelling. The Orthodox may continue to insist that the sole criterion of Jewishness is the sanction of talmudic masters because this is the divinely ordained criterion. True, this divine sanction itself rests upon rabbinical interpretation of scripture, so that belief in rabbinic authority rather than in revelation is really the ultimate dogma. But linguistic niceties will never prevail before passionately held conviction which itself has the sanction of that tradition. In addition, the Orthodox position may become increasingly less troublesome if American Judaism continues to define itself in religious rather than in communal-ethnic terms. The problem for the Orthodox criterion of Jewish survival is, as we have seen, that the expression of Jewishness overlaps one's secular mode of life. In other words, the Jewish component of one's life is not compartmentalized, whereas rabbinical authority is. Consciously or unconsciously, the fact of his Jewishness permeates the Jew's response to political, social, cultural, and family life; it has consequences for occupational choice, social mobility, and status.

But to say that this has always been true is not to suggest that conditions might not change. An increasingly religious self-definition by Jews may very well move the reality of being Jewish closer to the myth of the American Jewish experience. We have already suggested that age and occupation are playing an increasingly greater role in forging a person's identity. If Judaism should in fact become an American religion, then the Orthodox problem will be resolved. If the exclusive mode of Jewish identity is confined to the religious realm, then rabbinical authorities will be able to assert totalistic claims in determining what is or is not authentically Jewish.

The question is whether such a Judaism could survive. The answer is, probably not; but if any Jewish group could survive it would be the Orthodox. In the absence of a strong religious impulse or of societal support for religious affiliation, Jewishness may become increasingly bothersome. If one does have strong religious and Jewish inclinations, no institution provides a better outlet for their expression than does Orthodoxy.

An interesting and related question is whether Orthodoxy could survive without the non-Orthodox Jew. One may beg this question by suggesting that it is only Orthodoxy which permits the non-Orthodox definition and expression of religious Judaism. One might argue, for example, that in the situation where Judaism is increasingly defined religiously, non-Orthodox institutions may continue only as variants of Orthodoxy. That is, some Orthodoxy may be implicitly accepted as the expression of normative Judaism, and Conservatism or Reform defined by the aspects in which it demurs from Orthodoxy's ritualistic, dogmatic, or institutional norms. In fact, one could argue that in its elitist formulation, that is precisely what Conservative Judaism always has been and what Reform is becoming.

Nevertheless, it is unfair not to recognize the important and perhaps critical contribution that the non-Orthodox have made to Orthodox survival and to the quality of Orthodox life. At one time the non-Orthodox served as intermediaries between Orthodoxy and the general society. State control which enforced ritual supervision of meat products, laws protecting Sabbath observers in schools or at work, zoning ordinances permitting erection of synagogues, and favorable judicial interpretation of certain statutes were secured largely through the efforts of the non-Orthodox. This is no longer true. As a result of their acculturation and greater political sensitivity, the Orthodox no longer require non-Orthodox mediation. In fact, the most critical governmental issue today for the Orthodox is state aid to Jewish schools. On this issue the Orthodox are aligned with Catholics, and their bitterest opponents are the non-Orthodox.

The Orthodox may no longer require the non-Orthodox as intermediaries but they need them in other ways. Many Orthodox educational institutions are dependent on the financial support of non-Orthodox Jews. In addition, Orthodox Jews have been dependent upon non-Orthodox institutions for the expression of a broader Jewish identity. This must not be exaggerated; nor is the fact that this was true in the past necessarily a prediction for the future. But, at least until recently, fraternal organizations such as B'nai B'rith or landsmanschaft groups provided an important social and philanthropic outlet for many Orthodox as well as non-Orthodox Jews. The Zionist Organization of America enrolled many Orthodox Jews, and the religious Zionist organization in America took its cues from the larger nonreligious Zionist world. Within its own confines, Orthodox camping, improvement in curriculum materials and methods in Jewish schools, the little teacher training that exists, concern with aesthetic aspects of ritual and worship, the structure and organization of the modern synagogue, the meaningful involvement of women in Orthodox life—all owe a debt to the initiative of the non-Orthodox or to the fact that the non-Orthodox acted as a kind of filtration system from developments in the secular world to Orthodoxy.

Finally, the existence of non-Orthodox institutions provided an alternative to the hundreds of thousands and perhaps millions of Jews who rejected Orthodoxy and who, in the absence of an alternative, would have simply disappeared from Jewish life. Given the social and kinship ties between Orthodox and non-Orthodox Jews, the assimilation of the non-Orthodox would have had critical consequences to Orthodoxy's morale and family stability. Of course, many Orthodox believe that in the absence of non-Orthodox religious alternatives the main body of American Jews would have remained in the Orthodox fold. But all the evidence we have seems to contradict this.

Now let us return to our original question: Can Judaism survive in the United States? We have stated that an answer to the question requires some criterion of survival. We have suggested one such criterion which we labeled Orthodox. We have further noted that this criterion does not provide us with an adequate handle to evaluate the future of Judaism in the context of its contemporary expression. Let us turn to an alternative definition.

The Reform Position

The second possible criterion is nominal survival. As a matter of convenience we will label this position Reform, although many—perhaps most—Reform leaders would not accept it. According to this alternative, if we were transported into some future time, we could determine whether Judaism had survived by inquiring whether there were people who called themselves Jews. This definition avoids the problem of what is or is not in the Judaic tradition. It would certainly be congenial to those radical Reform theologians who argue that the only continuity in Judaism is one of accident. Even the more traditionalist theologians might argue that any group which chose to call itself Jewish necessarily stood in some continuity with contemporary Judaism.

There are, however, some problems with the Reform position. It would not help us resolve disputes between two groups, each of whom claimed to be Jewish but denied the legitimacy of the other's claim. The Reform criterion denies that any element within Judaism has the right to establish the boundaries of Judaism. But every group expresses its identity in the boundaries it establishes for itself. To deny a group the right to establish its own boundaries is tantamount to denying its right to exist as a meaningful social entity. There have been groups—some Negroes, for example—who have simply appropriated the name Jew for themselves and claimed to be the true descendants of the first Jews. Are they then to be admitted as Jews simply because they claim to be so? Contrary to the radical Reform theologians, most Jews do see themselves as part of a tradition that is more than nominal. If we rejected the first, or *Orthodox,* criterion as too limiting for the varied expression of American Judaism, we must reject this *Reform* criterion as far too open.

Most Jews believe that there is a traditional content to Judaism which still bears its original stamp. The fact of the matter is that early Palestinian and Babylonian Judaism—not to mention Spanish, and later German, Polish, and even Yemenite and North African Judaism—is clearly identifiable to the modern Jew. The Orthodox Jew of today might have trouble identifying the sanctums and lives of the classical Reform Jews as Jewish, but he would have no such trouble with any other Jewry in any other time. In fact, this may be one of the reasons Reform has resisted the sectarian impulses within its own ranks and moved more closely into conformity with the historical tradition. Surely, then, the criterion for Jewishness is more rigorous than a name. What if there was a community which met for prayer on Sunday, incorporated christological symbols, denied the validity of the Jewish code of law, and substituted new practices, but called itself Jewish or Israelite and had a leadership which could trace its Jewish ancestry back many generations? Would we call such a group Jewish? The example is not absurd. Indeed, it fits a description of the early Christian church. But, one may argue, the Christian church was different because it was juxtaposed to an existent normative Judaism. Would we therefore have to add that in order to be classified as Judaism, a group's members must both call themselves Jewish and be accepted as such by world Jewry? By whom in world Jewry? By its rabbinical leaders? Then we are back to the problems suggested by our first criterion. By some consensus of the Jewish people? Then we have really suggested a new and third alternative criterion.

The Conservative Position

Since we labeled the first criterion Orthodox and the second Reform, we will call the third Conservative. Like the others, this criterion does bear a relationship to some central ideas within Conservative Judaism, though not all Conservative Jews would necessarily subscribe to it. Under this definition we could determine whether Judaism had survived if its adherents were recognized as Jewish by some consensus of "the people of Israel" or "catholic Israel," as the term is sometimes used. This position implies that the Jewish people are somehow able to express their acceptance or rejection of a group's claim to Jewish authenticity.

There are two things to be said about this assertion. As the suggestion of a specific criterion it is utter nonsense. It tells us too little to settle cases in doubt. But it tells us enough to strike a resonant chord. The Conservative definition is not helpful in any actual controversy. In our own time, doubts have arisen about the Jewishness of individuals (Brother Daniel) and even total communities (the Bnei Israel of India, the Falasha Jews of Ethiopia, the Karaites—a Jewish sectarian group which resisted the rabbinical or oral law, though it accepted the authority of the Torah or written law—the Indian Jews of Mexico, and the Black Jews in the United States). The Jewish community has had to resolve the problem of their Jewishness and, except in the case of the Bnei Israel and the Falashas, there was no obvious consensus. The Conservative definition is too vague to be helpful in such cases. But though the definition is analytically useless, it nevertheless retains an appeal precisely because it fits the reality of Jewish self-perception. For the overwhelming majority of American Jews there is no difficulty in knowing whether they or most other people are Jewish. The quality that identifies them as Jews is felt as a continuity with the Jewish tradition. Most Jews are unable to define the tradition and are uncomfortable with efforts to do so, but this does not make a sense of Jewishness meaningless.

We may use an analogy here with the human race itself. We can only guess, and few of us care to guess about the manner in which the human race will evolve. It is possible for us to conceive of man a million years from now looking quite different from contemporary man (very short legs, very long arms, a huge cranium, eyes that rotate 180 degrees, no hair, and so on); yet we would recognize him as our successor. But let us assume that through evolution man evolved into a creature resembling a lizard and with the intelligence of a lizard. I think that if we were certain this was to occur most of us would believe that the human race was doomed, even if lizard-man was our true biological successor. The fact that we cannot specify precisely what the criteria for human survival are, the fact that we are not even able in marginal cases to decide a priori

whether this or that form of life constitutes a legitimate successor to us—all this does not mean that we have no sense of the
meaning of human survival.

DIMENSIONS OF SURVIVAL

At this point a more timid soul might end his speculation. We
began by asking whether American Judaism would survive. We
stated that to answer such a question we would first have to
determine the criteria for Jewish survival. What, in other
words, are the boundaries of Judaism beyond which we say
Judaism does not exist? We suggested three criteria and found
them all unsatisfactory. Lesser men might now conclude that
the question itself is unanswerable. We shall proceed with our
discussion, however, since our purpose is not to find a solution
but to illumine some aspects of Jewish life. The role of a Don
Quixote also has its compensations.

Sources of Immigration

Judaism might survive in the United States even if the present Jewish community had no biological successors. After all,
the present Jewish community bears little biological continuity
with the American Jewish community of 100 years ago and
almost none with the community of 150 years ago. Virtually all
the earliest Jewish immigrants, who were of Spanish descent,
have been totally assimilated, and the same is probably true for
most of the early German Jewish immigrants. It is conceivable
that the present Jewish community might disappear and a new
community arise from new sources of immigration. This, however, is unlikely. Barring some catastrophe to the State of Israel
which might bring large numbers of Jews from there to the
United States, there are possibilities of Jewish immigration from
the Soviet Union with two-and-one-half million Jews, or Latin
America with close to three-quarters of a million Jews. In addi-

tion, there are about half a million Jews in France and an almost equal number in Great Britain. Given the vagaries of Jewish history, one simply cannot dismiss the possibility of events which might permit or impel these Jews to emigrate.

But if we move from the realm of possibility to that of probability we must dismiss this as idle conjecture. Most American Jews have resisted assimilation pressures more than most French, English, or Russian Jews. (Obviously, pressures on Russian Jews were also far greater). Latin American Jewry has demonstrated a resistance to assimilation but lacks the internal resources to insure its survival. Should American Jewry voluntarily assimilate, it is doubtful that any major Jewish community outside the State of Israel would be likely to resist assimilation. Hence survival of American Judaism is dependent upon the biological continuity of the present Jewish community.

The Population Problem

Given the low birth rate among American Jews, and ignoring even the rising rate of intermarriage, some observers have questioned whether American Jews are reproducing themselves. But both fertility ratios and intermarriage rates are not irreversible. They are culturally determined and subject, at least to some extent, to an act of will on the part of American Jews. The biological question by itself is not, then, the ultimate question of Jewish survival. We may subsume it under the question of the will to survive—what price is the Jewish community willing to pay for survival? As we shall see, this still involves the biological question, not only as a problem of whether Judaism is reproducing itself, but also as an input in the increasing cost of remaining Jewish.

At the present time the Jews represent 2.6 percent of the total population, and that figure is declining. The lower the proportion of Jews in the population, the greater the survival costs become. It is reasonable to conjecture that self-pride and the will to survive of many Jews are related to their status in the large society. Political leaders today must take account of Jews, who constitute a respectable proportion of urban voters. Cultural institutions must take account of Jews, who constitute an important segment of their producers and consumers. Academic and intellectual groups are continually conscious of and sensitive toward Jews, who comprise such a large share of their community. Economic institutions must consider the Jews, who play a crucial role through their overrepresentation in professional and technical positions. Finally, as Marshall Sklare has pointed out, the Jew today, at the level of popular culture and belief, is not thought of as constituting 2.6 or even 3 percent of American society. The Jew is one-third of America. He has, after all, a one-third share in the Catholic-Protestant-Jew triumvirate which defines the religious composition of America. But we can go even further and give the Jew one-half share in the Judeo-Christian heritage upon which our secular society is presumably built.

But at what point does American society and its political, cultural, and economic institutions become conscious of the fact that Jewish status is discrepant with the Jewish composition of the society and its institutions? As the percentage of Jews in the total population continues to decline and as the proportion of non-Jews who attend college, enter the professions, earn above a certain amount of income, and so on increases, someone is going to wonder why Jews, the Jewish vote, Jewish sensitivity, and the like are to be taken so seriously. At that point, Jews will no longer be *in,* and the cost of being Jewish will rise. That day is unquestionably being hurried by Negro pressure to allocate rewards, prestigious jobs, and cultural concerns in accordance with one's proportion in the total population. Certain occupations—educational administration and social work, to mention two—are already sensitive to this pressure. Other institutions may soon follow. The Jewish biological problem is not, therefore, simply a question of whether Jews can reproduce themselves. It also relates to the relative status or position of the Jew in American society and hence the relative benefits or costs of being Jewish.

Jewish population may increase as a result of proselytization. A necessary condition would be that the Jewish community undertake positive efforts in this direction. Presently it is unwilling to do so. But even if the community reoriented its basic attitude, the effort is unlikely to be rewarded unless being Jewish means a great deal more than it now does; that is, unless being Jewish has a positive and significant meaning. This brings us back to the question of the quality of Jewish life, not the question of survival. The former problem has received much less attention that it deserves.

Other Aspects of Survival

Aside from the population problem there are other factors which will determine survival. Identifying these factors requires not only knowledge but also a great number of assumptions. For example, of the many factors which determine whether Judaism will survive in the United States one might assume that God's will is the primary factor. In that case, assuming also the accuracy of traditional Jewish notions about the operation of God's will, then the free choice of Jews concerning their ethical and ritual conduct will determine their future. Now, the fact that we wish to pursue our speculation along secular rather than religious lines really means that we are either ignoring God's will or making it a constant, while choosing to vary other factors. But this is a rather critical assumption. Factors which lend themselves more readily to scientific inquiry include economic, social, and political conditions in the United States, the degree and expression of anti-Semitism, the future direction of Black Power, the receptivity of American society to Negro demands, Negro-Jewish relations, America's international position and her relationship to Israel, Israel-Arab relations, the Jewish birth rate and intermarriage rates, the development of religion in America, the success or failure of the movement to further liberalize and Americanize the Catholic church,[2] the religious identification of American Jews, their relationship to Israel, and their definition of self and and mode of relationship to American society.

Obviously some of these variables are cause, others are effect. But distinguishing cause and effect itself involves certain assumptions. Evaluating the prospects of Jewish survival involves intelligence we do not possess. But our evaluation is also a function of our *belief* system concerning God, the nature of Judaism, and human behavior. It will not help at all to say that we make everything a constant. Even if we define the dimensions already specified more rigorously and assume they are the only relevant dimensions, our belief system would also dictate the trends for each of these dimensions. The identification of anti-Semitism and research into its relative increase or decrease depends on the definition one gives to anti-Semitism. This in turn depends on one's belief about its nature and source. Finally, we have the problem of reality yielding to our definition. Certainly, at least to some extent, the future of American Judaism is a function of how Jews perceive that future. We cannot escape the dilemma which inheres in the fact that the survival of American Judaism depends in part on how we estimate the prospects for its survival. If one is committed to Jewish survival and believes that there is no prospect for Jewish survival in America, one may emigrate to Israel. But this act then has an effect on Jewish survival in the United States.

If one turns from purely theoretical concerns of interest to social scientists to normative concerns of the Jewish community, then estimating the possibilities of survival ought not to occupy the energy of the community. The problem, rather, is to articulate a vision of the nature of survival. The challenge before the community is not to determine whether survival is possible, but to determine the dimension of *meaningful* survival and whether that is possible at all in the United States.

A PERSONAL OBSERVATION ON JEWISH SURVIVAL

I have suggested that no readily identifiable, analytically satisfactory criteria exist within the community to judge Jewish survival. This does not mean that individual Jews do not espouse one set of criteria or another. Like many others, I also have a definition of Judaism which establishes criteria by which I can judge not only whether Jews have survived but also the quality of Jewish life. My first criterion or condition is a sense of peoplehood. In my opinion a community is not Jewish if its members do not sense a special feeling of unity with and responsibility for the physical and spiritual welfare of all other Jews, wherever they are or whatever else they may be. To be Jewish is to sense that Judaism transcends national, regional, racial, and cultural boundaries and that one has special loyalties to other people outside of one's nation, region, or culture. A second aspect in my definition of Judaism is Torah. I understand Torah, at its least, to mean that a Jew must submit himself to a set of laws and practices which exist objectively or in a reality which is not of his construction. Torah is outside of us and calls upon us for an affirmation to which we must respond. If my community or I fail to respond, then we are bad Jews. But if the community, in its collective sense, denies the existence of Torah, then we are not Jews. The third aspect in my definition of Judaism is Jewish education as the study of Torah and sacred texts. This implies the belief that not only are some texts sacred but also that as a Jew one has special obligations to study and transmit them to others as sacred.

I would not call any community Jewish if any of these three qualities or characteristics were lacking. It does seem to me that all three are threatened today in the United States. The threat

is implicit rather than explicit, and hence all the more dangerous.

Jewish peoplehood is threatened by cosmopolitanism and
universalism, by the vision of an undifferentiated and diffuse
love and the desire to destroy all that separates men. It is hard
to argue against unity and love, hard to maintain the belief that
more lasting unity and love may come through each community's fulfilling the best in its own tradition, rather than
through cutting itself off from its roots.

Torah and the study of sacred texts are absurd in a society
which stresses the primacy of conscience and individual freedom against even society's own laws. The very notion of sacred
texts is antiquarian and outmoded. There is no room for a tradition of study when modern culture finds the very term sacred
to be anachronistic and affirms the value of activity, as against
the value of study, the relativism of all laws and values, and the
individual as the final arbiter of right and wrong.

Judaism, as I understand it, is threatened by contemporary
currents in American life. Fewer and fewer areas today are
even neutral to Jewish values. Literature, theater, art, scholarship, politics—all seem to undermine what I consider to be the
essentials of Judaism. More than ever before, the values of integration and survival are mutually contradictory. At least until
we enter a postmodern world, it seems to me that Jewish survival requires a turning against the integrationist response.

NOTES

1. RELIGION AND COMMUNALISM

1. Gustav Mensching, "Folk and Universal Religion," trans. Louis Schneider, in *Religion, Culture and Society*, ed. Louis Schneider (New York: John Wiley & Sons, 1964), p. 255.
2. Fritz Kunkel, *Einfuhrung in die Charakterologie*, p. 58, cited in G. van der Leeuw, *Religion in Essence and Manifestation* (New York: Harper, Torch Books, 1963), 1:242.
3. S.N. Eisenstadt, *Israeli Society* (New York: Basic Books, 1967), p. 315.
4. For an illuminating discussion of the interrelationship between ethnicity and religion in traditional Judaism, see Mordecai M. Kaplan, *The Greater Judaism in the Making: A Study of the Modern Evolution of Judaism* (New York: Reconstructionist Press, 1960), pp. 30–60. Needless to say, one may demur from Kaplan's theological conclusions while appreciating the value of his sociological analysis.
5. For a general history of modern Judaism, see Howard Sachar, *The Course of Modern Jewish History* (Cleveland: World Publishing Company, 1958).
6. Stephen M. Poppel, "Jewish Identity and the Modern Jew," *Midstream* 14 (November 1968): 67. I am indebted to Poppel for his suggestion of three alternative criteria of modernity within what I call the sociointellectual approach.
7. Ernst Cassirer, *The Philosophy of the Enlightenment* (Boston: Beacon Paperback, 1955), pp. 13–14.

8. The forces within the Jewish community struggling for emancipation emerged, as we note, against a backdrop of a disintegrating Jewish community. There is no better book in English on the subject—indeed, no better book in the whole field of modern Jewish history—than Jacob Katz's *Tradition and Crisis* (New York: Free Press, 1961).

9. On the emancipation in Western Europe and the Jewish price for emancipation, see Jacob Katz, "The Term 'Jewish Emancipation': Its Origin and Historical Impact," Alexander Altmann, *Studies in Nineteenth Century Jewish Intellectual History* (Cambridge, Mass.: Harvard University Press, 1964), pp. 1–25; Jacob Toury, "The Jewish Question: A Semantic Approach," *Year Book XI of the Leo Baeck Institute* (London: Leo Baeck Institute, 1966), pp. 85–106; Arthur Hertzberg, *The French Enlightenment and the Jews* (New York: Columbia University Press, 1968); and Michael A. Meyer, *The Origins of the Modern Jew: Jewish Identity and European Culture in Germany, 1749–1824* (Detroit: Wayne State University Press, 1967).

10. On the emancipation of Jews in Central Europe there are some articles of interest in Randolph L. Braham, ed., *Hungarian Jewish Studies* (New York: World Federation of Hungarian Jews, 1966), and *The Jews of Czechoslovakia*, vol. 1 (Philadelphia: Jewish Publication Society, 1968).

11. On the emancipation of East European Jewry, see Louis Greenberg, *The Jews in Russia*, 2 vols. (New Haven: Yale University Press, 1944); and Simon H. Dubnow, *History of the Jews in Russia and Poland*, 3 vols. (Philadelphia: Jewish Publication Society, 1920).

12. Salo Wittmayer Baron, *Modern Nationalism and Religion* (New York: Meridian Books, 1960), p. 223.

13. Ibid., p. 241.

14. On the 1937 Aguda Convention, see Hillel Seidman, "Likrat T'kumat HaMedina," *Tora u'Mlucha*, ed. Shimon Federbush (Jerusalem: Mosad Hakov Kook, 1951), pp. 228–46.

15. Nathaniel Katzburg, "Hungarian Jewry in Modern Times: Political and Social Aspects," Braham, ed., *Hungarian Jewish Studies*, p. 140.

16. Ibid., p. 141.

17. *The Jews of Czechoslovakia*, vol. 1.

18. Aharon Moshe Rabinowicz, "The Jewish Minority," ibid., pp. 198–99.

19. Hugo Stransky, "The Religious Life in the Historic Lands," ibid., p. 331.
20. Gustav Fleischmann, "The Religious Congregation, 1918–1938," ibid., p. 322.

2: INTEGRATION AND SURVIVAL

1. For anecdotal evidence from Boston, see Herman Rubenovitz and Mignon Rubenovitz, *The Waking Heart* (Cambridge, Mass.: Nathaniel Dame and Co., 1967), p. 27.
2. Theodor Herzl, *The Jewish State* (New York: American Zionist Emergency Council, 1946), p. 90.
3. Chaim Weizmann, "The Jewish Problem in the World," *Israel among the Nations: Selection of Zionist Texts*, ed. Zvi Zohar (Jerusalem: World Zionist Organization, 1966), p. 136.
4. *Jewish Post and Opinion*, 31 May 1968, p. 1.
5. Such a response would find allies among other Jews who are only sensitive to the threat to their own economic welfare, or who might themselves be prejudiced against Negroes. Our focus, however, as we indicated, is not so much with the content of one's position, but how one arrives at a position.
6. Quoted in *Jewish Post and Opinion*, 6 October 1967, p. 3, cited in Geraldine Rosenfield, *Interim Report on the New Left and Alienated Youth* (New York: The American Jewish Committee Information Service, December 1967), p. 32.
7. *New York Times*, 20 November 1967, p. 30, cited in ibid.
8. There is an alternative integrationist response from a right-wing political perspective, but this is less common among Jews, for reasons to be noted in chapter 7.
9. Rosenfield, *Interim Report*, p. 34.
10. *New York Times*, 27 July 1968, p. 28.

3: THE RELIGION OF AMERICAN JEWS

1. To the reader concerned with theoretical niceties we might add the following bibliographic digression. Our first definition of folk religion was based on an article by Gustav Mensching, cited in chapter 1. An article by E. Wilbur Bock, "Symbols in Conflict: Official versus Folk Religion," *Journal for the Scientific Study of Religion* 5 (Spring 1966): 204–12, uses that and another article by Mensching to distinguish *folk* from *official* religion. Our present

definition of *folk* and *elite* is informed by, though not identical to, Bock's definitions. The reader who so wishes may trace the relationship between our definition of folk religion in chapter 1 and the definition we shall outline here. For the less ambitious, it is just as easy to consider the present set of definitions as different from and unrelated to those in chapter 1.

2. This discussion follows O'Dea's treatment of institutional religion, in which he distinguishes three levels: cult, belief, and organization; Thomas O'Dea, *The Sociology of Religion* (Englewood Cliffs, N.J.: Prentice-Hall, 1966), pp. 36–51.

3. Samuel S. Cohon, "The History of Hebrew Union College," *Publications of the American Jewish Historical Society* 40 (September 1950): 24.

4. Judah David Eisenstein, *Ozar Zikhronothai* (New York: Published by the author, 1929), pp. 206–11. The pages are reprinted from an article by Eisenstein in the *New York Yiddish Zeitung,* 1886.

5. The text of the Pittsburgh Platform is reprinted in Nathan Glazer, *American Judaism* (Chicago: University of Chicago Press, 1957), pp. 151–52.

6. The distinction and some application to contemporary Judaism is made by Jacob Katz, "Traditional Society and Modern Society," *M'Gamot* 10 (March 1960): 304–11 (Hebrew).

7. Agudat Horabbonim, *Jubilee Volume* (New York: Arius Press, 1928), p. 110.

8. Cited in Abraham J. Karp, "New York Chooses a Chief Rabbi," *Publications of the American Jewish Historical Society* 45 (March 1955): 129–98.

9. Ezekial Lifschutz, "Jewish Immigrant Life in American Memoir Literature," *YIVO Annual of Jewish Social Science* 5 (1950): 232.

10. Shlomo Noble, "The Image of the American Jew in Hebrew and Yiddish Literature in America, 1870–1900," ibid. 9 (1954): 87. A Yiddish story relates how Jews in a small East European town raised money to send a young man to America to prevent him from marrying a Gentile; Isaac Metzker, "To the New World," *A Treasury of Yiddish Stories,* ed. Irving Howe and Eliezer Greenberg (New York: Meridian Books, 1958), pp. 504–15. Milton Himmelfarb has noted: "After all, who went to America? Overwhelmingly, it was not the elite of learning, piety, or money but the *shnayders,* the *shusters* and the *ferdgenevim";* Milton Himmelfarb, "The Intellectual and the Rabbi," *Proceedings of the Rabbinical Assembly of America,* 1963, p. 124. See also Mark Zborow-

ski and Elizabeth Herzog, *Life Is with People* (New York: Schocken Books, 1952), pp. 260–61, and Arthur Hertzberg, "Seventy Years of Jewish Education," *Judaism* 1 (October 1952): 361.

11. Moshe Davis, "Jewish Religious Life and Institutions in America," *The Jews: Their History, Culture, and Religion*, 2d ed., ed. Louis Finkelstein (Philadelphia: Jewish Publication Society, 1955), 1, 539. See also Bernard D. Weinryb, "Jewish Immigration and Accommodation to America: Research, Trends, Problems," *The Writing of American Jewish History*, ed. Moshe Davis and Isidore Meyer (New York: American Jewish Historical Society, 1957), p. 319, for a similar point.

12. Lloyd P. Gartner, *The Jewish Immigrant in England, 1870–1914* (Detroit: Wayne State University Press, 1960), p. 30.

13. Cited in Moses Rischin, *The Promised City* (Cambridge, Mass.: Harvard University Press, 1962), pp. 146–47.

14. Gartner, *The Jewish Immigrant*, p. 195.

15. Alexander M. Dushkin, *Jewish Education in New York City* (New York: Bureau of Jewish Education, 1918), p. 21.

16. Ibid., p. 156.

17. Agudat Horabbonim, *Jubilee Volume*, p. 16.

18. Moses Weinberger, *Ha-Yehudim Vehayahadut B'New York* (New York: 1887), p. 2.

19. Eugene Markovitz, "Henry Pereira Mendes, 1880–1920" (Ph.D. diss., Yeshiva University, 1961), p. 136.

20. Cited in Glazer, *American Judaism*, p. 73.

21. Marshall Sklare, *Conservative Judaism* (New York: Free Press, 1955), pp. 161–65, 191–93.

22. Ibid.

23. Abraham J. Karp, *A History of the United Synagogue of America, 1913–1963* (New York: United Synagogue of America, 1964), p. 9.

24. Charles S. Liebman, "The Variety of Conservative Jews" (Unpublished report for the United Synagogue of America).

25. Stanley K. Bigman, *The Jewish Population of Greater Washington in 1956* (Washington, D. C.: Jewish Community Council of Greater Washington, 1957); Fred Massarik, *A Report on the Jewish Population of Los Angeles, 1959* (Los Angeles: Jewish Federation Council of Greater Los Angeles, 1959); Sidney Goldstein, *The Greater Providence Jewish Community: A Population Survey* (Providence: General Jewish Community of Providence, 1964); Albert J. Mayer, *Social and Economic Characteristics of the Detroit Jewish Community: 1963* (Detroit: Jewish Welfare Federation of Detroit, 1964); idem, *Milwaukee Jewish Population Study*,

1964–1965 (Milwaukee: Milwaukee Jewish Welfare Fund, 1967); and Morris Axelrod, Floyd J. Fowler, and Arnold Gurin, *A Community Survey for Long Range Planning: A Study of the Jewish Population of Greater Boston* (Boston: Combined Jewish Philanthropies of Greater Boston, 1967).

26. The Los Angeles data are for 1959. Between 1951 and 1959 the percentage of Jews in Los Angeles identifying themselves as Conservative went up from 20 percent to 35 percent. The proportion of Orthodox, Reform, and nonidentifiers decreased. This trend may very well continue, so that the distribution of Jews by religious groups in Los Angeles will resemble other centers of Jewish population in the United States.

27. Sklare, *Conservative Judaism,* p. 217.

28. Ibid., p. 67.

29. Moshe Davis, *The Emergence of Conservative Judaism* (Philadelphia: Jewish Publication Society, 1963).

30. Marshall Sklare and Joseph Greenblum, *Jewish Identity on the Suburban Frontier* (New York: Basic Books, 1967), and studies of Jews in Miami, Baltimore, Kansas City, and White Plains, conducted by Manheim Shapiro for the American Jewish Committee.

31. Gerhard Lenski, *The Religious Factor,* rev. ed. (New York: Doubleday, Anchor Books, 1963), p. 37.

32. Sklare and Greenblum, *Jewish Identity,* pp. 269–90.

33. Ibid., pp. 271–72.

34. Ibid., pp. 280–81.

35. Werner J. Cahnman, "Comments on the American Jewish Scene," in *Conference on Acculturation,* ed. Herbert Strauss (New York: American Federation of Jews from Central Europe, 1965), pp. 20–21. For the theoretical discussion underlying this phenomenon, see Milton Gordon, *Assimilation in American Life* (New York: Oxford University Press, 1964).

36. Herbert I. Gans, "The Origin and Growth of a Jewish Community in the Suburbs: A Study of the Jews of Park Forest," *The Jews: Social Patterns of an American Group,* ed. Marshall Sklare (New York: Free Press, 1958), pp. 217–18.

37. Ibid., p. 217.

38. *National Census of Jewish Schools,* American Association for Jewish Education Information Bulletin no. 28. (December 1967).

39. Ibid.

40. *Survey of Synagogue Membership* (New York: United Synagogue of America, 1965).

41. Axelrod, Fowler, and Gurin, *A Community Survey*, p. 139.
42. Ibid., pp. 122, 137.
43. For the sources, see note 25. The city with the highest percentage of Jews reporting that they attended synagogue services more than once a month was Milwaukee, with 29 percent so reporting. For other cities the figures were Providence: 21 percent; Los Angeles: 18 percent (once a month or more); Boston: 17 percent; Washington, D. C.: 14 percent.
44. Axelrod, Fowler, and Gurin, *A Community Survey*, p. 135.
45. Bernard Lazerwitz, *A First Report on the General Components and Consequences of Jewish Identification*, mimeographed (Waltham, Mass.: National Jewish Welfare Board, 1968), p. 19. Similar conclusions are to be found in Bigman, *Jewish Population of Greater Washington*, p. 68, and Axelrod, Fowler, and Gurin, *A Community Survey*, p. 165.
46. First published in 1934 by Macmillan, the volume has been reprinted by the Reconstructionist Press and most recently (1967) by Schocken Books in a paper edition.
47. David Philipson, *My Life as an American Jew* (Cincinnati: John G. Kidd & Son, 1941), p. 128.
48. See chapter 5 for details of this survey.
49. For a detailed discussion of types of Orthodox Jews and Orthodox institutions, see Charles S. Liebman, "Orthodoxy in American Jewish Life," *American Jewish Year Book, 1965*, ed. Morris Fine and Milton Himmelfarb (Philadelphia: Jewish Publication Society, 1965), pp. 21–97. Part of this discussion also draws upon my article "A Sociological Analysis of Contemporary Orthodoxy," *Judaism* 13 (Summer 1964): 285–304.
50. Robert Lee, *The Social Sources of Church Unity* (Nashville: Abingdon Press, 1960).
51. For details of the study, see Charles S. Liebman, "Changing Social Characteristics of Orthodox, Conservative and Reform Jews," *Sociological Analysis* 27 (Winter 1966): 210–12.

4: AMERICAN JEWS AND ISRAEL

1. Marshall Sklare and Joseph Greenblum, *Jewish Identity on the Suburban Frontier* (New York: Basic Books, 1967), p. 322.
2. The article, in which a full copy of the questionnaire and a lengthy discussion of its results are reproduced, is Charles S. Liebman, "Reconstructionism in American Jewish Life," *American Jew-*

ish Year Book, 1970, ed. Morris Fine and Milton Himmelfarb (Philadelphia: Jewish Publication Society, 1970), pp. 3–99. The article in the *Year Book,* however, devotes relatively little attention to the responses on questions about Israel. This is discussed more fully in Yesha'yahu (Charles) Liebman, "The Role of Israel in the Ideology of American Jewry," *Unity and Dispersion* 10 (Winter 1970): 19–26.

3. Charles Herbert Stember et al., *Jews in the Mind of America* (New York: Basic Books, 1966).
4. For an excellent illustration of this mentality, see the letter by Rabbi Balfour Brickner in *Commentary* 51 (June 1971): 8–12.
5. Sklare and Greenblum, *Jewish Identity,* pp. 231–34.
6. Ibid., pp. 233–34.
7. Nathan Rotenstreich makes a similar point in his comments in *Changing Relationships between Israel and the Diaspora* (Jerusalem: Institute for Contemporary Jewry, Publications of the Study Circle on Diaspora Jewry, 1969), pp. 60–61 (Hebrew).
8. At the time of writing I could only find a copy of the Hebrew translation which appeared in *Tefutsot Israel* 8 (November–December 1970): 31–33.

5: RABBINICAL STUDENTS

1. See, for example, Isaac Metzker, ed., *A Bintel Brief: Sixty Years of Letters from the Lower East Side to the Jewish Daily Forward* (Garden City, N.Y.: Doubleday, 1971).
2. Norman Podhoretz, *Making It* (New York: Random House, 1967), pp. 109–36.
3. From the foreword by Joseph Schlossberg to Samuel Kurland, *Cooperative Palestine,* cited in Mordecai M. Kaplan, *A New Zionism* (New York: Herzl Press, 1959), p. 89.
4. The full report of the survey is found in Charles S. Liebman, "The Training of American Rabbis," *American Jewish Year Book 1968,* ed. Morris Fine and Milton Himmelfarb (Philadelphia: Jewish Publication Society, 1968), pp. 3–112.
5. On the rabbi's role, see Arthur Hertzberg, "The Changing American Rabbinate," *Midstream* 12 (January 1966): 16–29.
6. Respondents were asked to check, on a list of fifteen, which problem they felt deserved highest priority. Those that received at least one check were grouped as follows: religious problems—the state of Jewish belief, the decline of religious observance and

ritual practice, and the intellectual challenges to Judaism; ethnic-communal problems—Soviet Jewry, the strength and survival of Israel, anti-Semitism, intermarriage, assimilation, and Jewish college youth; other problems—the social and ethical values of American Jews and Jewish education. Students were also given an open-ended option, but no one suggested any problems other than those listed.

7. Respondents were asked to check the aspect of the rabbinate that appeared most attractive to them from a list of twelve items. Those aspects that were checked at least once were grouped as follows: religious aspects—the opportunity to help people find faith, the opportunity to make people more observant, and the opportunity to teach Torah; other aspects—the opportunity to serve as a leader in the general community, the opportunity for social action, the opportunity to preserve Judaism, the opportunity to serve as a leader in the Jewish community, the opportunity to study and think, and comfortable living conditions. There was also an open-ended question. The few responses in this category were included under "other aspects."

6: JEWISH YOUTH

1. Bernard Rosen, *Adolescence and Religion* (Cambridge, Mass.: Schenkman Publishing Co., 1965), pp. 73, 178–84.
2. Ibid., p. 182. See also Irving Jacks, "Attitudes toward Interfaith Heterosexual Socializing in a Group of Jewish Teenagers," *Review of Religious Research* 9 (Spring 1968): 182–88. Jacks found sharp differences in attitudes between Orthodox, Conservative, and Reform youths. For example, 82 percent of the Orthodox and only 35 percent of the Reform thought that in order to be a good Jew it was essential that a person marry within the Jewish faith.
3. *A Study of Jewish Adolescents of New Orleans* (New Orleans: Jewish Welfare Federation of New Orleans, 1966), p. 22.
4. Ibid.
5. Ibid., p. 23.
6. Ibid., pp. 19–20.
7. Ibid., p. 53.
8. Marshall Sklare and Marc Vosk, *The Riverton Study* (New York: American Jewish Committee, 1957), pp. 13–16.
9. Ibid., p. 29.

10. Ibid., p. 26. Bernard Rosen, in his studies of Jewish youth, phrased his question somewhat differently. He found that 46 percent of his respondents thought that a person was a Jew by virtue of his being born of Jewish parents, rather than by virtue of his religion. But even among those who felt that way, 17 percent stated that a person born of Jewish parents but who does not believe in any religion is not a Jew. The reader should bear in mind that under Jewish law, a child born of a Jewish mother is Jewish; Rosen, *Adolescence and Religion*, pp. 171-72.
11. Sklare and Vosk, *The Riverton Study*, p. 28.
12. Rosen, *Adolescence and Religion*, p. 171.
13. Ibid., p. 74.
14. *A Study of Jewish Adolescents*, p. 37.
15. Ibid., p. 20.
16. Ibid., p. 54.
17. Ibid.
18. Ibid., p. 13.
19. Rosen, *Adolescence and Religion*, pp. 157-58.
20. Ibid., p. 53.
21. Ibid., p. 104.
22. Ibid., pp. 97-104.
23. *A Study of Jewish Adolescents*, p. 36.
24. David Boroff, "Jewish Teen-Age Culture," *Annals of the American Academy of Political and Social Science* 338 (1961): 79-90.
25. *A Study of Jewish Adolescents*, p. 26.
26. Charles Y. Glock and Rodney Stark, *Religion and Society in Tension* (Chicago: Rand McNally, 1965), p. 271.
27. Ibid., pp. 276-78.
28. Ibid., p. 277.
29. Daniel R. Miller and Guy E. Swanson, *The Changing American Parent* (New York: John Wiley & Sons, 1958), p. 293.
30. See Bill Novak and Robert Goldman, "The Rise of the Jewish Student Press," *Conservative Judaism* 25 (Winter 1971): 5-19.

7: JEWISH LIBERALISM

1. Some recent studies which compare Jewish and non-Jewish attitudes and behavior with respect to party preference or political issues, or both, include Gerhard Lenski, *The Religious Factor*, rev. ed. (New York: Doubleday, Anchor Books, 1963), pp. 134-68, 210; Lawrence Fuchs, *The Political Behaviour of American Jews*

(Glencoe, Ill.: Free Press, 1956); idem, "American Jews and the Presidential Vote," *American Political Science Review* 49 (June 1955): 385–401; Edgar Litt, "Status, Ethnicity, and Patterns of Jewish Voting Behaviour in Baltimore," *Jewish Social Studies* 22 (July 1960): 159–64; Samuel A. Stouffer, *Communism, Conformity and Civil Liberties* (Garden City, N.Y.: Doubleday, 1955), p. 113; Angus Campbell et al., *The American Voter* (New York: John Wiley & Sons, 1960) pp. 159, 301, 306; Wesley Allinsmith and Beverly Allinsmith, "Religious Affiliation and Politico-Economic Attitudes," *Public Opinion Quarterly* 12 (Fall 1948): 377–89; Lucy S. Dawidowicz and Leon J. Goldstein, *Politics—A Pluralist Democracy* (New York: Institute of Human Relations Press, 1963); Lloyd A. Freeland and Hadley Cantril, *The Political Beliefs of Americans* (New York: Simon and Schuster, 1968), pp. 145–49.

2. Of course, these social facts do not occur randomly. They themselves have been attributed to certain Jewish traditions, values, or distinctive group conditions. See, for example, Nathan Glazer, "Social Characteristics of American Jews, 1654–1954," *American Jewish Year Book, 1955,* ed. Morris Fine and Milton Himmelfarb (Philadelphia: Jewish Publication Society, 1955), pp. 3–41.

3. Campbell et al., *The American Voter,* pp. 301–6.

4. Angus Campbell and Homer G. Cooper, *Group Differences in Attitudes and Votes* (Ann Arbor: University of Michigan, Survey Research Center, 1956), p. 23.

5. Ibid., p. 44.

6. Ibid., p. 63.

7. On Jewish support for Wallace, see, for example, Fuchs, "American Jews and the Presidential Vote," p. 387, and Samuel Lubell, *The Future of American Politics,* rev. ed. (New York: Doubleday, Anchor Books, 1957), pp. 218–27.

8. Campbell and Cooper, *Group Differences,* p. 135.

9. Fuchs, "American Jews and the Presidential Vote," p. 392.

10. Lenski found the same phenomenon in the vote for Michigan governor. Jews and Negro Protestants were unaffected by the candidacy of a Catholic, whereas Catholics favored him and Protestants rejected him; Lenski, *The Religious Factor,* pp. 145–46.

11. Nathan Glazer and Daniel Patrick Moynihan, *Beyond the Melting Pot,* (Cambridge, Mass.: M.I.T. Press, paperback edition, 1964), pp. 305–9. See also Edward Costikyan, *Behind Closed Doors* (New York: Harcourt, Brace and World, 1966). Costikyan believes the Jews rejected Morgenthau in reaction to the publicity over the

poll. Even if true, this supports our contention. It indicates much about how Jews think they ought to behave politically. Catholics were not materially affected by the preelection announcements by pollsters that they were going to support Kennedy overwhelmingly.

12. Ibid., p. 309.
13. Dawidowicz and Goldstein, *Politics*, pp. 77-78.
14. John H. Fenton, *The Catholic Vote* (New Orleans: Hauser Press, 1960), pp. 78-83.
15. Fuchs, *Political Behaviour of American Jews*. The relevant sections here are reprinted in Marshall Sklare, ed., *The Jews: Social Patterns of an American Group* (Glencoe, Ill.: Free Press, 1958), pp. 595-613.
16. For a theological abstraction of these values which are not entirely identical to those of Fuchs but which, in their author's opinion, serve as key components of religious belief that distinguish political conservatism from political liberalism, see Michael Parenti, "Political Values and Religious Cultures," *Journal for the Scientific Study of Religion* 6 (Fall 1967): 268.
17. Charles S. Liebman, "Religion, Class, and Culture in American Jewish History," *The Jewish Journal of Sociology* 9 (December 1967): 227-41.
18. The point is nicely developed in Erich Fromm, *You Shall Be as Gods* (New York: Holt, Rinehart and Winston, 1966).
19. See, for example, Philip E. Converse, "The Nature of Belief Systems in Mass Publics," *Ideology and Discontent*, ed. David Apter (New York: Free Press, 1964), pp. 206-61. On the specific point stressing the discontinuity between theological beliefs and political attitudes or behavior, see Benton Johnson and Richard H. White, "Protestantism, Political Preference, and the Nature of Religious Influence: Comment on Anderson's Paper," *Review of Religious Research* 9 (Fall 1967): 28-35.
20. Charles Y. Glock and Rodney Stark, *Religion and Society in Tension* (Chicago: Rand McNally, 1965), pp. 18-38; Yoshio Fukuyama, "The Major Dimensions of Church Membership," *Review of Religious Research* 3 (Spring 1961): 154-61; Morton King, "Measuring the Religious Variable," *Journal for the Scientific Study of Religion* 6 (Fall 1967): 173-90. See also other articles on this subject in the same issue.
21. Morris Axelrod, Floyd J. Fowler, and Arnold Gurin, *A Community Survey for Long Range Planning: A Study of the Jewish Popula-*

tion of Greater Boston (Boston: Combined Jewish Philanthropies of Greater Boston, 1967).

22. Charles S. Liebman, "The Training of American Rabbis," *American Jewish Year Book, 1968*, ed. Morris Fine and Milton Himmelfarb (Philadelphia: Jewish Publication Society, 1968), pp. 3–112.

23. Nathan Glazer, *American Judaism* (Chicago; University of Chicago Press, 1957), pp. 137–38; Joseph Zeitlin, *Disciples of the Wise: The Religious and Social Opinions of American Rabbis* (New York: Teachers College, Columbia University, 1945), pp. 29–38.

24. Zeitlin, *Disciples of the Wise.*

25. This study was conducted in 1965 under a grant from the Memorial Foundation for Jewish Culture. The full results are as yet unpublished. The responses were based on a 35 percent return.

26. Edgar Litt, "Jewish Ethno-Religious Involvement and Political Liberalism," *Social Forces* 39 (May 1961): 328–32.

27. Seymour Martin Lipset, *Political Man* (Garden City, N.Y.: Doubleday, Anchor Books, 1963), p. 256. See also Allinsmith and Allinsmith, "Religious Affiliation."

28. A somewhat similar theory to account for the disproportionate number of Jews in the American Communist party is found in Nathan Glazer, *The Social Basis of American Communism* (New York: Harcourt, Brace and World, 1961), pp. 130–68. Glazer, however, stresses that whereas Jews comprised the most important segment of the Communist party, only a very small fraction of American Jews were Communists. His theory differs from the theory of status inferiority by accounting for Jewish communism in terms of the late entry of the Jews into certain professions, which resulted in their being the first to suffer during the Great Depression.

29. Edgar Litt, "Ethnic Status and Political Perspectives," *Midwest Journal of Political Science* 5 (August 1961): 278.

30. Ibid., p. 280. Further evidence against the status-inferiority theory is found in Edward O. Laumann and David R. Segal, "Status Inconsistency and Ethnoreligious Group Membership as Determinants of Social Participation and Political Attitudes," *American Journal of Sociology* 77 (July 1971): 36–61.

31. Werner Cohn, "The Politics of American Jews," in Sklare, ed., *The Jews*, pp. 614–26. See also Dawidowicz and Goldstein, *Politics*, pp. 78–81, who attribute major significance to this theory in accounting for Jewish liberalism.

32. Jacob Toury, "Emancipation and Assimilation," *Moreshet* 2 (1964): 167–82 (Hebrew).
33. Bernard R. Berelson et al., *Voting* (Chicago: University of Chicago Press, 1954), pp. 71–72.
34. Fuchs, "American Jews and the Presidential Vote," p. 390.
35. Litt, "Jewish Ethno-Religious Involvement and Political Liberalism," p. 330.
36. Fuchs, "American Jews and the Presidential Vote," p. 393.
37. We do not argue that no radical Socialist has ever maintained Jewish commitments. Indeed, there have been Jewish radical Socialist parties. But the radical Socialists did not recognize the legitimacy of such ideologies, and, as in the Soviet Union, they have ended by turning violently against such Jewish parties. By the same token, we do not deny the existence of a liberalism stemming from authentic Judaic values. We would argue, however, that this is not a widespread phenomenon and that an additional or external factor is necessary to explain the choice of the liberal rather than the conservative option that also exists within the tradition.
38. See, for example, Carl Becker, *The Heavenly City of the Eighteenth-Century Philosophers* (New Haven: Yale University Press, 1932).
39. Quoted in Fuchs, *The Political Behaviour of American Jews*, p. 121.
40. Ibid., p. 57.
41. Cited in ibid., p. 53.
42. Cited in ibid., p. 58.
43. The material on Teddy Roosevelt and the 1912 election comes from ibid., pp. 51–60.
44. I am relying here on my own observations as a campaign worker in the primary.
45. Richard E. Morgan, *The Politics of Religious Conflict* (New York: Pegasus, 1968), p. 122.
46. Ibid.
47. Jean-Paul Sartre, *Anti-Semite and Jew*, trans. George Becker (New York: Schocken Books, 1948), pp. 23–24.
48. Cited in ibid., p. 24.
49. See the excellent essay on this by Milton Himmelfarb, "Secular Society? A Jewish Perspective," *Daedalus* 96 (Winter 1967): 220–36.
50. Jacob Toury, "The Jewish Question: A Semantic Approach," *Year*

Book XI of the Leo Baeck Institute (London: Leo Baeck Institute, 1966), pp. 97–98.

51. Ibid.

52. Albert Memmi, *The Liberation of the Jew* (New York: Orion Press, 1966), p. 236.

53. Bernard K. Johnpoll, *The Politics of Futility: The General Jewish Workers Bund of Poland, 1917–1948* (Ithaca: Cornell University Press, 1967).

54. This quest, it seems to me, has possible reflections even in the methodology, interests, and pursuits of the Jewish academician. Given the disproportionate number of Jews in the academic disciplines, one might be led to inquire why no one has ever bothered to ask whether they can be distinguished from non-Jews in their choice of fields, in their methodology, or in the conclusions they draw from their research. A reasonable hypothesis would seem to be that behaviorism and relativism are methodologies and attitudes particularly congenial to Jews. I don't wish to press the hypothesis in the absence of data. But the entrance of large numbers of Jews into the various social sciences in the past twenty years seems to be coterminous with radical changes in the pursuits of these disciplines. As a behaviorist (and a liberal) I can testify to having been quite unselfconscious about my academic methodology, but I suspect that this would have to be the case. Otherwise I would be defeating the very universalism I espouse. Universalistic Jewish values are not tricks the Jews play on society. At worst, they are tricks the Jews play on themselves. For an interesting essay along somewhat similar lines, see Thorstein Veblen, "The Intellectual Pre-Eminence of Jews in Modern Europe," reprinted in *Essays in Our Changing Order* (New York: Viking Press, 1934), particularly pp. 225–30. More direct support for the suggestion advanced here is a chapter by Etienne Gilson, "The World of Secular Learning," in his *The Philosopher and Theology* (New York: Random House, 1962), pp. 20–41. Writing about his Jewish professors at the Sorbonne at the turn of the century, he says: "The doctrines of these university professors were really quite different from one another. Even the personal philosophy of Levy-Bruhl did not coincide exactly with that of Durkheim, while Frederic Rauh was going his own way. . . . The only element common to their doctrines is a negative one, but nonetheless real and very active in its own order. One might describe it as a radical defiance of all that which is social conceived as a constraint from

which to be liberated. Spinoza and Brunschvieg achieved this liberation through metaphysics. Durkheim and Levy-Bruhl through science and sociology, Bergson through intuition" (pp. 31–32).

8: RADICAL JEWISH STUDENTS AND THE JEWISH FAMILY

1. Robert H. Somers, "The Mainsprings of the Rebellion: A Survey of Berkeley Students in November, 1964," *The Berkeley Student Revolt,* ed. Seymour Martin Lipset and Sheldon S. Wolin (Garden City, N. Y.: Doubleday, Anchor Books, 1965), p. 548.
2. Richard Flacks, "The Liberated Generation: An Exploration of the Roots of Student Protest," *The Journal of Social Issues* 23 (July 1967): 65.
3. James W. Trent and Judith L. Craise, "Commitment and Conformity in the American College," ibid., p. 40.
4. William A. Watts and David Whittaker, "Free Speech Advocates at Berkeley," *The Journal of Applied Behavioral Science* 2 (January, February, March 1966): 54.
5. Flacks, "The Liberated Generation," pp. 60, 70.
6. See, for example chapter 7 of this book and articles by S. Joseph Fauman, Nathan Glazer, Fred Strodtbeck, Jackson Toby, Charles Snyder, Lawrence Fuchs, and Werner Cohn in *The Jews: Social Patterns of an American Group,* ed. Marshall Sklare (New York: Free Press, 1958).
7. Martha Wolfenstein, "Two Types of Jewish Mothers," ibid., pp. 520–34.
8. These points were made in lectures by Sklare and subsequent conversations which it was my privilege to share with him.
9. Fred Strodtbeck, "Family Interaction, Values and Achievement," *The Jews,* ed. Sklare, p. 156.
10. *New York Times,* 19 May 1968 , p. 1.
11. Ibid., p. 84.
12. Flacks, "The Liberated Generation," pp. 66–68.
13. Ibid., p. 68.
14. Ibid., p. 65.
15. *Jewish Post and Opinion,* 31 May 1968, p. 1. See chapter 2 for a further discussion.
16. Flacks, "The Liberated Generation," p. 70.
17. For a fuller development of this argument see Marshall Sklare, "The Values of East European Jewry and of American Society," *Jewish Frontier* (July 1961): 7–11.

18. Trent and Craise, "Commitment and Conformity," pp. 38-39.
19. I am indebted to Abraham Duker for this thought.
20. Glen Lyonns, "The Police Car Demonstration: A Survey of Participants," Lipset and Wolin, *The Berkeley Student Revolt*, pp. 519-30. However, we should also note that by the time the questionnaires were distributed, events had served to increase militancy among the student activists and increase significantly the number willing to risk arrest and expulsion. (Unfortunately, the two quite different risks were coupled in the same question.)

9: SOME OBSERVATIONS ON THE FUTURE OF AMERICAN JUDAISM

1. Jacob Neusner, "Rabbis and Community in Third Century Babylonia," *Religions in Antiquity: Essays in Memory of Erwin Ramsdell Goodenough*, ed. Jacob Neusner (Leiden: E. J. Brill, 1968), pp. 438-59.
2. This reference deserves some elaboration. The Catholic church is undergoing liberalization, challenges to authority, and a breakdown of its own particularism. Should the trend continue, it will increase the pressure upon Jews to surrender aspects of their own religious particularism.